THE BIRTH CONTROL BOOK

The
BIRTH CONTROL
BOOK

A Complete Guide
to Your Contraceptive Options

SAMUEL A. PASQUALE, M.D.
AND JENNIFER CADOFF

BALLANTINE BOOKS
New York

Copyright © 1996 by Samuel A. Pasquale, M.D., and Jennifer Cadoff

All rights reserved
under International and Pan-American Copyright Conventions.
Published in the United States by Ballantine Books,
a division of Random House, Inc., New York,
and simultaneously in Canada by Random House
of Canada Limited, Toronto.

The authors have used many brand names and product names in this book.
All are trademarks or registered trademarks of their respective companies.
All efforts have been made to follow correctly the capitalization style used
by the manufacturers of such products to distinguish them from generic or
descriptive terms. However, the use or inadvertent misuse in this text of brand
names or product names should not be regarded as affecting the validity of
any trademark or service mark.

Samuel A. Pasquale, M.D., has been involved in contraceptive research and
development for more than thirty years. During that time he has consulted
for or received research grants from a number of organizations whose products
may be mentioned in this book, including the Population Council; Organon,
Inc.; Ortho-McNeil Pharmaceutical; and Wyeth-Ayerst Laboratories.

http://www.randomhouse.com

Library of Congress Cataloging-in-Publication Data
Pasquale, Samuel A.
The birth control book : a complete guide to your contraceptive options /
Samuel A. Pasquale and Jennifer Cadoff.
p.   cm.
Includes index.
ISBN 0-345-40037-2
1. Contraception—Popular works.   2. Birth control.
I. Cadoff, Jennifer.   II. Title.
RG136.2.P37   1996
613.9'4—dc20   96-10807

Manufactured in the United States of America

First Edition: July 1996

10 9 8 7 6 5 4 3 2 1

9/96 B&T 7.20

This book is meant to educate and should not be used as an alternative to appropriate medical care. The authors have exerted every effort to ensure that the information presented is accurate up to the time of publication. However, because the research and reporting of information about birth control is ongoing, it is possible that new findings may invalidate some of the information presented here. Ultimately, each reader is responsible for obtaining complete and current information about the risks, benefits, and efficacy of birth control methods and seeking, where appropriate, the services of a licensed health care professional.

We dedicate this book to our families:
Carole, Chris, Martha, Greg, & Stuart
Evan, Rebecca, & Eli

CONTENTS

INTRODUCTION

What This Book Is About . . . And How to Use It   *I*

PART ONE

HOW TO CHOOSE A CONTRACEPTIVE

1   *Zeroing in on the Right Birth Control Method*   *9*

2   *Body Basics*   *27*

3   *Talking to Your Doctor About Birth Control*   *38*

PART TWO

"NATURAL" BIRTH CONTROL

4   *Fertility Awareness Methods*   *49*

PART THREE

BARRIER METHODS

5   *Condoms*   *63*

6   *Female Condoms*   *72*

7   *Vaginal Spermicides*   *81*

8   *Diaphragms*   *89*

9   *Cervical Caps*   *101*

PART FOUR
HORMONE-BASED METHODS

10 Oral Contraceptives—"The Pill"   115

11 Progestin-Only "Minipills"   133

12 Norplant—Under-the-Skin Contraception   143

13 Depo-Provera—"The Shot"   156

PART FIVE
INTRAUTERINE DEVICES

14 IUDs   169

PART SIX
STERILIZATION

15 Tubal Ligation   183

16 Vasectomy   193

PART SEVEN
CONTRACEPTIVE FAILURE

17 When Birth Control Fails   203

PART EIGHT
FUTURE CONTRACEPTIVES

18 What's on the Birth Control Horizon?   217

GLOSSARY   235

APPENDIX
Where to Go for More Information   247

INDEX   254

WHAT THIS BOOK
IS ABOUT . . .
AND HOW TO USE IT

There are currently more than 69 million women in the United States between the ages of fifteen and fifty, the span of life commonly referred to as the childbearing years. About half of those women, 34 million or so, are now using some type of reversible contraceptive, according to the Ortho 1995 Annual Birth Control Study. (The rest are either using no method or are no longer fertile because of voluntary sterilization, hysterectomy, or menopause.)

Thirty-four million women. Women just like you, who want and *need* to know all they can about birth control.

Yet, choosing a contraceptive—one that is the best possible match for your age, personality, health, lifestyle, and future childbearing plans—is not an easy thing to do. A lot of us make decisions about birth control somewhat haphazardly, asking a doctor for a pill prescription because of a best friend's recommendation, for example, or shying away from IUDs because we've read about disasters that occurred with the Dalkon Shield years ago. Sometimes, too, we stick with a birth control method for far too long, well after we've "out-grown" it, and would like to switch to something else—if only we could figure out what might work better.

The goal of this book is to make picking a contraceptive a simpler, clearer, and more straightforward process—whether it's the first time you will be doing so or the second or the third. It will help you make a decision based on solid facts and on your needs as an individual, instead of on outdated myths, half-truths, and misunderstanding. Once you have selected a birth control method, this book will also provide you with information that can make your contraceptive as effective and easy-to-use as possible.

There are many birth control options these days, and many factors to consider when you're trying to weigh the advantages of one against another. To help get you started on the right track, part one of *The Birth Control Book* is set up to help you figure out which contraceptive method—or methods—might be good choices for you. You will consider such factors as how easy or difficult it might be to use various types of birth control, how effective they are at preventing pregnancy, whether or not they provide protection against sexually transmitted diseases, and much more.

In this first section there's also a brief overview of the menstrual cycle, since understanding your body's natural rhythms of fertility is an important part of choosing and using birth control effectively.

Finally, there is a chapter aimed at making it easier to talk to your doctor about contraception. While it is true that you don't need a doctor's prescription for some types of birth control (such as condoms and spermicides), it is still a very good idea to talk to your physician (family practitioner or gynecologist) or a health care professional at a family planning clinic before you start to use *any* method of birth control, or before you stop using a method that you aren't happy with. It is also very important that young women see a family planning professional *before* they become sexually active. It is all too easy to get pregnant accidentally—sometimes even the very first time you have sex—if you find yourself unprepared in the heat of the moment.

The second section of *The Birth Control Book*—parts two through six—devotes a full chapter to each type of contraceptive that is currently available in the United States and, method by method, describes what it is, how it works, where to get it, how to use it, who can and who shouldn't use it, and its advantages and disadvantages. The more you know about all types of birth control, the more likely you will be to choose a method you can live with successfully.

In this section of the book contraceptives that work in basically similar ways are grouped together to make it easier for you to compare them. For example the "barrier contraceptive" section includes the chapters on condoms and diaphragms, and the section on "hormonal methods" covers everything from birth control pills to Norplant (the relatively new implants-in-your-arm contraceptive).

The information in each of the chapters on the individual contraceptives is presented in exactly the same way, with subheads designating "what it is," "how it works," "who is a good candidate for this method," and so on. This should also help make comparisons between methods easier. If, for example, "effectiveness" or "cost" are particular concerns, you can easily flip from one chapter to another, find the relevant sections, and zero in on precisely the information you're looking for.

* * *

The final sections of the book—parts seven and eight—offer additional information about specific issues relevant to birth control. The chapter on "contraceptive failure" deals with what your options are if, like so many women each year, you should find yourself in this difficult situation. The chapter on "future contraceptives" outlines the progress being made in research into new birth control methods and devices, including when they might become available. Finally, there is also a glossary, where you can find definitions of all the technical and medical terms used throughout the book, and an appendix, which lists further sources of information on various topics.

The information contained in this book is as accurate, complete, and up-to-date as possible. When something is not known for sure, we will say so; if a topic is controversial, we'll let you know that; if there isn't good research to support some of the often-repeated "facts" about birth control (something that happens more than you might think), we will make that clear.

Statistics have been compiled from recognized and respected medical journals, such as *Contraception, Family Planning Perspectives*, and the *New England Journal of Medicine,* and from sources like the National Survey of Family Growth (which offers the most comprehensive nationwide information available on birth control), the Ortho Annual Birth Control Study (which is conducted yearly by Ortho-McNeil Pharmaceutical), the *Physicians' Desk Reference* (or PDR, which contains, among other things, a compilation of the package inserts for most of the prescription drugs available in this country), *Contraceptive Technology* (a professional's handbook that has been referred to as "the bible of birth control"), the American College of Obstetricians and Gynecologists (ACOG), and the Population Council and the Alan Guttmacher Institute, both nonprofit organizations devoted to research on family planning issues.

However, because new scientific studies and new research are published on birth control every day, it is inevitable that some of the information contained in these pages may be a bit out of date by the time you read it. Also, in spite of our diligent efforts to be accurate, it is always possible that errors may inadvertently slip by us. These are more good reasons to talk to your doctor about a birth control method before you start to rely on it. If you read an article in the newspaper, or see something on the TV about late-breaking birth control news, only someone who knows you—your health history, your age, your personal circumstances—can explain how, or even if, this newfound information might apply to you. And if we report that something is true for "most people," your doctor or health care provider is the one who can tell you if it holds true for you, too.

Part One

❧

HOW TO
CHOOSE A
CONTRACEPTIVE

CHAPTER

1

ZEROING IN ON THE RIGHT BIRTH CONTROL METHOD

This is a book about options. It is based on the premise that there is no single method of contraception that is right for every woman. There is also no single method that will continue to be right for any one woman throughout her reproductive years.

Today there are more kinds of birth control to choose from than ever before. There are options that weren't even available in this country just a few years ago—such as the female condom, Depo-Provera, and Norplant. In addition, ongoing research and technological advances have transformed many "old" contraceptives, such as the Pill and the IUD, making them excellent choices for more women than ever before. Even some "natural" approaches to preventing pregnancy have gotten quite sophisticated these days. These techniques do not expose women to hormones and chemicals, but they do require considerable commitment and a solid base of knowledge about fertility if they are to be used effectively.

Many women are unhappy with the contraceptive they

now use. If you are one of them, chances are good that you will be able to find a method that will work better for you, once you have all the facts you need at your fingertips. Without the facts, you might choose a contraceptive because one particular aspect of it sounds appealing, or because your best friend uses it—but that method might be a poor choice for you for any number of other reasons. Conversely you might not even consider a particular method that could be an excellent choice for you, simply because your mother or a friend had a bad experience with it, or because you saw or read an unfavorable story about it in the news.

In some ways the sheer number of options available today can, in and of itself, make picking the right contraceptive harder. Condoms, spermicides, diaphragms and cervical caps, pills and shots and implants, IUDs, and sterilization. From this almost bewildering array, how can you zero in on the single method that is right for you, right now? How can you know when it's time to change your method—since, as we have said, no single contraceptive will be the right choice for a woman throughout her childbearing years. If you're forced to stop using a particular contraceptive—due to health problems, say, or a change in lifestyle—how can you decide what to try next? How can you make a truly informed decision?

Consider the Methods You've Tried in the Past

One good place to start is to take a minute to think about all of the contraceptives you've ever used—why you chose the methods you did, what you liked and disliked about each of them, and what made you stop using one method and switch to another.

Think About What's Most Important to You

There are a number of factors to consider when you're choosing a method of birth control. They include the following:

- The method's *effectiveness*
- Its *cost*
- Your *personality* and *lifestyle*
- Your *stage in life*
- Your *fertility*
- Your *risk of sexually transmitted diseases* (STDs)
- Your *partner's attitude toward birth control*
- Your *health*

EFFECTIVENESS

Birth control methods vary tremendously in how well they prevent unintended pregnancies. For example, fewer than one woman in one hundred will get pregnant in a year of using either the ParaGard IUD or Depo-Provera injections; compared with about twelve condom users in one hundred and approximately eighteen women out of every one hundred who choose the diaphragm. How much risk are you comfortable with? Exactly how sure do you need to be, for your own peace of mind, that you won't get pregnant? Have you thought about what you would do if you did have an unplanned pregnancy? This isn't an easy issue to consider, but it should be a part of your contraceptive decision making.

The chart on the next page shows how often women become pregnant accidentally when they're using the various methods of birth control. You may be surprised, when you look at it, to see how certain methods rate. You may also be surprised by how big a difference there is between the most effective and the least effective methods.

Percentage of women experiencing a contraceptive failure during the first year of typical use and the first year of perfect use and the percentage continuing use at the end of the first year, United States

METHOD	% of Women Experiencing an Accidental Pregnancy within the First Year of Use		% of Women Continuing Use at One Year
	TYPICAL USE	PERFECT USE	
(1)	(2)	(3)	(4)
Chance	85	85	
Spermicides	21	6	43
Periodic Abstinence	20		67
Calendar		9	
Ovulation Method		3	
Sympto-Thermal		2	
Post-Ovulation		1	
Withdrawal	19	4	
Cap			
Parous Women	36	26	45
Nulliparous Women	18	9	58
Sponge			
Parous Women	36	20	45
Nulliparous Women	18	9	58
Diaphragm	18	6	58
Condom			
Female (Reality)	21	5	56
Male	12	3	63
Pill	3		72
Progestin Only		0.5	
Combined		0.1	
IUD			
Progesterone T	2.0	1.5	81
Copper T 380A	0.8	0.6	78
LNg 20	0.1	0.1	81
Depo-Provera	0.3	0.3	70
Norplant (6 Capsules)	0.09	0.09	85
Female Sterilization	0.4	0.4	100
Male Sterilization	0.15	0.10	100

Emergency Contraceptive Pills: Treatment initiated within 72 hours after unprotected intercourse reduces the risk of pregnancy by at least 75%.

Lactational Amenorrhea Method: LAM is a highly effective, *temporary* method of contraception.

(Hatcher RA, Trussell J, Stewart F, Stewart GK, Kowal D, Guest F, Cates W, Policar MS. Contraceptive Technology, New York: Irvington Publishers, Inc., 1994)

Another very important thing to notice about this chart is that it has two separate columns, one listing pregnancy rates for "typical use" and the other for "perfect use." For some methods—look at condoms, for example—there's a big difference between the numbers in those two columns. Typically, if one hundred couples used condoms for one year, twelve women would get pregnant. If, on the other hand, those one hundred couples used this method perfectly—*exactly according to instructions every time they had sex*—just three women in one hundred would be expected to get pregnant. For other methods, such as Norplant, the numbers in the two columns are exactly the same. Why? Because once the tiny hormone-filled tubes are implanted in a woman's upper arm, it is impossible to "forget" or misuse this method.

COST

Here, too, the range is enormous. Norplant implants cost about $360, a diaphragm about $20 (not including a doctor's office visit in either case). Two methods that cost virtually the same when averaged out over time can hit your pocketbook very differently. For example, Norplant and tubal ligation (female sterilization) and vasectomy (male sterilization) are all quite expensive, and you have to pay for them up front. (Some of the cost may be covered by insurance.) With methods like condoms and spermicides, on the other hand, you pay as you go, buy only as much as you need, and only when you need it. We have included a cost-comparison chart (page 14) so that you can see some of the differences at a glance.

Cost of contraceptive methods, based on assumption of 100 acts of intercourse annually

METHOD	UNIT COST ($)	ANNUAL COST ($)	COMMENTS
Cervical Cap	20 plus 50–150 for fitting	Cost of spermicide: 85	
Male Condom	0.50	50	Add cost of spermicide if used
Female Condom	2.50	250	Add cost of spermicide if used
Diaphragm	20 plus 50–150 for fitting	Cost of spermicide: 85	
Depo-Provera	35/injection	140	
IUD	120 plus 40–50 for insertion/ lab tests	160 for Progestasert; 20 for Cu T 380A if retained 8 years*	
Norplant	350/kit plus 150–250 for insertion/removal	130–170 if retained 5 years*	5-year cost: 650–850
Pill	10–20/cycle	130–260	
Spermicides	0.85/application	85	
Sponge	4/pack of 3	133	

*Norplant and Cu T 380A have considerably higher annual costs if devices are removed prior to expiration; however, Wyeth Laboratories will refund cost of implants if removed before 6 months.

(Hatcher RA, Trussell J, Stewart F, Stewart GK, Kowal D, Guest F, Cates W, Policar MS. Contraceptive Technology, New York: Irvington Publishers, Inc., 1994)

PERSONALITY AND LIFESTYLE

A lot of what you should consider when it comes to your lifestyle and personality is directly linked to the issue of "perfect use" versus "typical use," because some methods of birth control are a lot easier to use correctly than others.

Are you the type who can remember to take a birth control pill every single day? Would you really be willing and able to take your temperature every morning before you get out of bed, as one "natural" method requires? Do you have the discipline to put in your diaphragm or Reality condom every time you have sex? If you are fairly orderly, detail oriented, and motivated, you probably will remember to take your pills, and you might even enjoy the challenge of tracking your temperature as a means of natural fertility control. If, on the other hand, you are more spontaneous or the type who always loses her keys, you are probably less likely to do well with these methods.

Now consider the other end of the convenience spectrum: Would you be thrilled to simply go to the doctor for a shot of Depo-Provera every three months and basically forget about birth control in between? Or what about having Norplant's six tiny tubes of hormone implanted in your upper arm to prevent pregnancy for up to five years? If convenience is a top priority, you could even choose a ParaGard IUD, which, once inserted, works for up to ten years.

Some women don't like to take pills. If you're one of them, you're not going to do well on oral contraceptives, no matter how perfect a match this method might be otherwise. Similarly if you hate shots, Depo-Provera is not for you. Some women don't feel comfortable touching themselves, so the diaphragm or cervical cap would not be good choices for them. There is no right or wrong here. The only issue is how well a particular method suits *you*.

Consider your schedule and the demands of your school or work. If, for example, your job requires a lot of long-distance travel or changing shift hours, it may be hard for you to take birth control pills regularly. (They work best when taken as close to once-every-twenty-four-hours as possible.) If you have a baby or small children, you know that irregular hours and unpredictable schedules come with the territory, so your birth control choice should be as simple and foolproof as possible. If you and your partner have sex mostly on weekends, maybe a cervical cap (which can be left in place for forty-eight hours) would be the perfect choice; while the daily hormone dose of Norplant or Depo-Provera, or even the Pill, might strike you as contraceptive overkill.

· STAGE IN LIFE

Most women should expect to use several different types of contraception during their reproductive lifetimes. After all, this is quite a span of years when you think about it, stretching from your first period, at about age eleven, to your last, at about age fifty-two.

Typically women will probably go through three basic stages during their childbearing years:

- *The early years of sexual activity.* During this stage, women are at peak fertility (so they need a highly effective method), but they're often not yet ready to have children (so they also tend to be concerned about finding a method that has a low risk of jeopardizing their ability to conceive in the future). They may also need to be wary of sexually transmitted diseases, including AIDS.

- *The childbearing years.* At this stage you may need a contraceptive that is safe to use while you're nursing a baby, for example, or one that's readily reversible so that you can stop and start using it easily between planned pregnancies.

- *After kids.* At this point in life you've had all the children you want, but you're still fertile and still sexually active.

You might now opt for a method that wouldn't have been a consideration earlier, such as tubal ligation, or vasectomy for your partner.

These days of course there are practically as many variations on this basic theme as there are individual women. The first stage might last until your late thirties, if you haven't found the right man or if you're putting off having kids to concentrate on your career. You might decide you never want to have children. On the other hand you might marry your high school sweetheart, have three kids in your twenties, and be done with childbearing by the time you're thirty. Or you might have gotten divorced, fallen in love again, and be eager to have more children. No matter what path you end up traveling in life, however, the point remains the same: What you will look for in a contraceptive is likely to be quite different when you're eighteen or twenty-three than it is when you're thirty-five, and different again when you're forty-five.

The chart on the following pages shows how popular various methods are among women at different ages. Condoms, for example, are used most frequently by younger women. Sterilization steadily gains users as women get older. The Pill is most popular with women in the middle of their childbearing years.

FERTILITY

There are a number of factors that determine how fertile you are; that is, how likely you are to get pregnant. Your age is just one of them. (In general, fertility is highest from about the late teens to the midthirties, declines slowly until age forty or so, then drops more quickly after that.)

Other factors that indicate how likely you are to be fertile include the following:

The Popularity of Various Birth Control Methods by Age of User

PERCENTAGE OF WOMEN AT RISK OF PREGNANCY, 1988

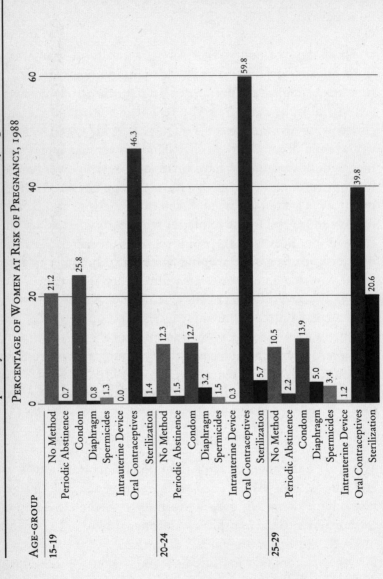

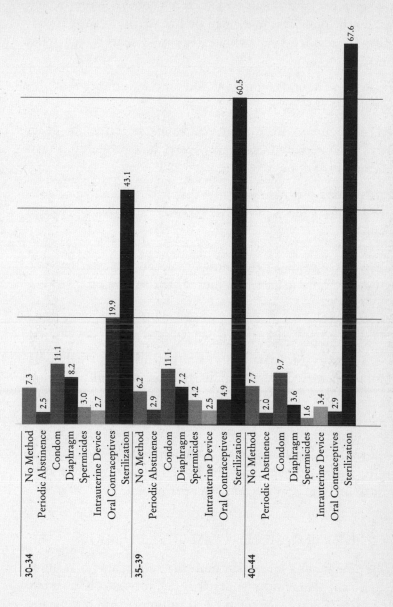

30-34							
No Method	7.3						
Periodic Abstinence	2.5						
Condom	11.1						
Diaphragm	8.2						
Spermicides	3.0						
Intrauterine Device	2.7						
Oral Contraceptives	19.9						
Sterilization	43.1						

35-39	
No Method	6.2
Periodic Abstinence	2.9
Condom	11.1
Diaphragm	7.2
Spermicides	4.2
Intrauterine Device	2.5
Oral Contraceptives	4.9
Sterilization	60.5

40-44	
No Method	7.7
Periodic Abstinence	2.0
Condom	9.7
Diaphragm	3.6
Spermicides	1.6
Intrauterine Device	3.4
Oral Contraceptives	2.9
Sterilization	67.6

(Reproduced with permission of the Alan Guttmacher Institute from Susan Harlap, Kathryn Kost, and Jacqueline Darroch Forrest, Preventing Pregnancy, Protecting Health: A New Look at Birth Control Choices in the United States, New York, 1991)

■ Sex more often than two or three times a week, which increases the odds that there will be live sperm in your reproductive tract when you ovulate (release a mature egg from your ovaries).

■ Regular periods, which would tend to indicate that you are ovulating regularly.

■ Intercourse with a man you know is fertile. In other words if he's fathered children before, he's probably physically capable of doing so again.

■ Previous pregnancy. While this is no guarantee of continued fertility, it does show that you were able to get pregnant in the past.

Conversely some of the things that can indicate that you may be less likely to conceive include the following:

■ Infrequent sex
■ Skipped periods, irregular bleeding
■ A history of sexually transmitted disease or pelvic inflammatory disease, which can cause infertility
■ A history of infertility or a condition such as polycystic ovarian syndrome that is a known cause of infertility

The more factors you have that would tend to indicate high fertility, the more you need a highly effective method of contraception if you don't want to get pregnant.

RISK OF SEXUALLY TRANSMITTED DISEASES

Unless you are in a long-term mutually monogamous relationship, you should consider yourself at risk for sexually transmitted diseases (STDs). If you have sex with more than one person, *or if your partner has sex with others,* and even if you only have sex with one person at a time, it is critical that you know whether your method of birth control provides protection against STDs.

Everyone is at risk for STDs. It doesn't matter how rich or poor you are, or whether you live in the city, the suburbs, or out in the country. Teenagers having sex for the first time get STDs, as do forty-year-old widows and divorcées who, until now, had never had sex with anyone but their ex-husbands. Don't bury your head in the sand: With more than 12 million cases of sexually transmitted diseases occurring in this country every year, STDs are common, and they are definitely not something that only happens "to the other guy."

Many STDs have few or subtle symptoms, so you can't count on being able to look at a man and tell if he's "clean." You certainly can't take a new partner's word for it, at least not until you know him well enough to know that you can really trust him. (And in this age of AIDS, how much does it take to trust someone with your life? An impossible question that each woman must answer for herself.)

You can get an STD if you have sex just once with someone who has one. In most cases women become infected more easily than men—that is, STDs are passed more easily from men to women than vice versa (see chart on page 24). In addition the consequences of infection are often much more serious for women. Some strains of human papillomavirus (HPV), which can cause genital warts, have been linked to cervical cancer. STDs such as chlamydia and gonorrhea can cause pelvic inflammatory disease, which can permanently scar the fallopian tubes and result in infertility. Herpes is incurable; and it can, in some cases, cause serious infections in babies born to women with active outbreaks. And then there's AIDS, which as everyone knows by now, is both incurable and a killer.

Sexually Transmitted Diseases: More Common Than Most People Think

Estimated Millions of Americans with These Health Problems

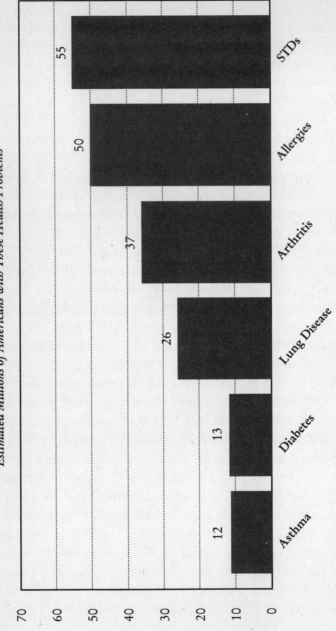

STDs	55
Allergies	50
Arthritis	37
Lung Disease	26
Diabetes	13
Asthma	12

(The American Social Health Association)

PARTNER'S ATTITUDE TOWARD BIRTH CONTROL

Another thing you need to consider is how much control you want to have over your birth control method. Obviously if you plan on using condoms, you have to have a willing partner. But even with a method like the Pill, a man can exert considerable influence over a woman to stop taking it—sometimes subtly, with comments about weight gain or acne, sometimes more directly.

In fact it sometimes seems as if men have nothing but complaints about birth control. Condoms reduce sensation. They bump into the rim of the diaphragm, or get poked by the string of the IUD. Spermicide makes the woman's vagina too slippery, or it irritates the skin on his penis. They complain about the irregular periods that can occur with Norplant (if either they or their partners don't want to have sex when the woman is bleeding).

In some cultures it's seen as a sign of manhood to get a woman pregnant. Men raised in this type of environment may be actively against a woman's use of birth control. (Of course men aren't always the bad guys: If a woman wants to get pregnant over the objections of her partner, it's easy enough for her to "accidentally on purpose" forget a pill or two.)

The man's attitude probably won't be the deciding factor in most women's choice of a birth control method. However, since a partner can make a significant difference in how consistently you use certain methods, it is definitely something to think about.

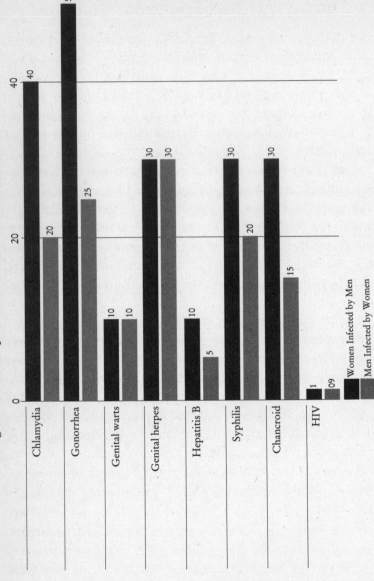

Estimated Percentage of Women and Men Becoming Infected During One Act of Unprotected Intercourse with an Infected Person

	Women Infected by Men	Men Infected by Women
Chlamydia	40	20
Gonorrhea	50	25
Genital warts	10	10
Genital herpes	30	30
Hepatitis B	10	5
Syphilis	30	20
Chancroid	30	15
HIV	1	09

(Reproduced with permission of The Alan Guttmacher Institute from Susan Harlap, Kathryn Kost, and Jacqueline Darroch Forrest, Preventing Pregnancy, Protecting Health: A New Look at Birth Control Choices in the United States, New York 1991)

HEALTH

Many women have medical conditions—such as diabetes, hypertension, obesity—that limit their choice of contraceptives. IUDs, for example, are not recommended for women with conditions that compromise their ability to fight off infection, including AIDS. A woman who has had a stroke, blood-clotting problems, or certain cancers should not be on oral contraceptives. Conversely the Pill might be a good choice for a woman with a family history of ovarian or endometrial (uterine lining) cancer, since there is good scientific evidence that it can significantly reduce the risk of these malignancies.

These and many other health and medical considerations will be discussed in greater detail, as they apply, in the chapters on individual contraceptives.

Zeroing in on the best contraceptive choice is often a matter of balancing the pros against the cons of several contenders, because just as there is no contraceptive method that's right for every woman, there is also no perfect contraceptive. Every method—even the most highly effective—has some failures. And every method—even the safest and simplest—has potential side effects and drawbacks.

Now that you have some idea of the things you need to think about in order to choose a contraceptive, you might want to try ranking which of these factors are the *most* important to you: effectiveness, cost, health and medical factors, safety and side effects, convenience, STD protection, preserving your future fertility, and how much control you want to have over your method. Then, armed with your personal priority list, you can focus on the issues that matter most to

Leading Contraceptive Methods

	1993 (%)	1994 (%)	1995 (%)
Sterilization	27	26	24
Tubal Ligation	15	15	15
Vasectomy	13	12	10
Pill	25	24	26
Condom	19	19	19
Withdrawal	6	5	6
Rhythm	3	3	3
Diaphragm	2	2	2
Sponge	2	1	1
Vaginal Suppository	2	1	1
Douche	1	1	1
Foam	1	1	1
IUD	1	1	1
Cream/Jelly alone	1	1	1
Cervical cap	*	*	*
Implant	1	1	1
Female Condom/Pouch	*	*	*
No method	19	19	20
Hysterectomy/Menopause	8	9	6
Pregnant	2	2	3
Trying to conceive	2	2	2

(Ortho-McNeil 1995 Annual Birth Control Study. Used by permission of Ortho-McNeil Pharmaceutical.)

you as you read about the various methods in the upcoming chapters.

Finally, we've included one more chart (see above). It shows you how popular various methods are today in the United States, and compares their use now to that in years past.

2

BODY
BASICS

To really understand how birth control methods work, and to be able to use them correctly, you have to know a bit about the female body—both its anatomy (where things are and what they're called) and its physiology (how things work).

Female Body Parts—What's Visible on the Outside

The entire external genital area is often referred to in medical terms as the *vulva*, a Latin word that means "covering."

In sexually mature women this area is almost completely covered by the pubic hair. The bony rise just above the genitals, where the pelvic bones come together, is called the *mons pubis*. The outer folds of hair-covered skin, which protect and cover the vaginal area, are called the *labia majora*, which means "large lips" in Latin. Inside the folds of the labia majora are smaller, highly sensitive folds of pinkish skin known as the *labia minora*, or "small lips." At the top of the labia minora, an inch or so in front of the opening to the vagina, is the extremely sensitive, small knob of flesh called the *clitoris*, which

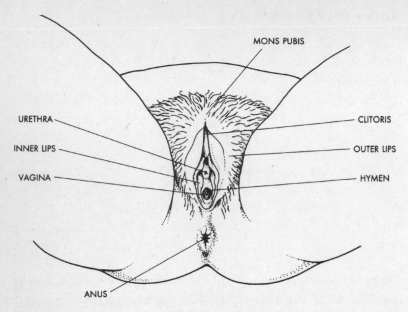

MONS PUBIS

URETHRA

INNER LIPS

VAGINA

CLITORIS

OUTER LIPS

HYMEN

ANUS

(Diana Korte, Every Woman's Body, *illustrations by Dana Burns-Pizer, New York: Ballantine, 1994)*

EXTERNAL GENITAL AREA

plays a central role in sexual pleasure for most, but not all, women. The ring of tissue around the vaginal opening is the *hymen.* The hymen varies a great deal from woman to woman—it can be relatively thick and tough, or quite thin and easily stretched, or even virtually invisible. Because of these normal variations a sexual partner can't tell whether a woman is a virgin by looking at her vaginal opening or by having sex with her. Even a doctor may not be able to tell during an examination.

The *anus,* which is the opening at the end of the intestinal tract, lies behind the vaginal opening. The opening of the *urethra,* the tube that carries urine from the bladder to the outside of the body, is between the vagina and the clitoris. This small slit is nearly invisible unless you gently pull its edges apart.

Inside the Female Body

In conspicuous contrast to the male reproductive system, most of the female organs of reproduction are on the inside of the body.

The *vagina* is the link between the external and internal organs of reproduction. In mature women the vagina is about four inches long and consists of soft, stretchy tissue that normally lies flat like a deflated balloon when there's nothing in it. During sexual excitement the walls of the vagina secrete lubricating fluid that allows the penis to slide into it more easily.

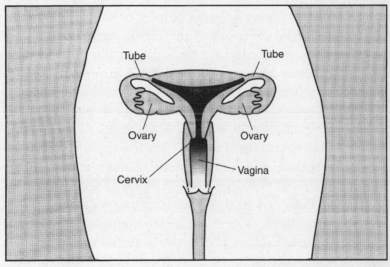

(AVSC International)

INTERIOR REPRODUCTIVE ORGANS

At the top, or internal end, of the vagina is the *cervix*, the narrow lower end of the *uterus* that juts out about an inch into the top of the vagina. You should be able to touch your cervix if you put a finger or fingers into the vagina and reach inward—it may feel like a rounded bulge, harder than the surrounding vaginal tissue, with a dimple in its center. (Some people say the cervix feels a bit like the end of your nose.) Women who use barrier methods of birth control, such as the diaphragm and cervical cap, need to be comfortable locating the cervix in order to check that these devices are in proper position.

The "dimple" in the cervix is the opening, or *os*, of the narrow canal that runs through the cervix from end to end. This canal opens and closes very slightly at different times of the menstrual cycle, and stretches wide during the delivery of a baby. Glands in the cervix produce most of the secretions that you may notice coming out of the vagina during the month. These secretions change with the ebb and flow of the menstrual hormones and can be used to help predict when a woman is fertile. (This will be discussed more in chapter 4, "Fertility Awareness Methods.") It is the cervix from which your doctor collects cells when he or she takes a Pap smear.

The entire *uterus*, or womb, is approximately pear-sized and pear-shaped, with thick muscular walls that have the ability to expand enormously when a baby is growing within it. In your body the pear is upside down, with the narrow end being the cervix. The inside of the nonpregnant uterus is triangle-shaped. Each of the top two angles of the triangle leads to one of the *fallopian tubes* (or *oviducts*); and the bottom point of the triangle is the cervical canal. The tissue that forms the inner lining of the uterus is known as the *endometrium*. The endometrium responds to the stimulation of hormones during the menstrual cycle, first growing thicker and full of glands and blood vessels, and then, if conception does not occur, sloughing off and flowing down through the cervix and vagina in menstruation.

The *fallopian tubes*, or *oviducts*, are the narrow passage-ways through which eggs travel on their way from the *ovaries* to the uterus. There is one tube on each side of the uterus; each is about four inches long. The far end of the tubes do not attach directly to the ovaries. Instead fine fingerlike projections, called *fimbria*, at the end of each tube catch the egg when it is released from the ovary and sweep it into the tube. The walls of the fallopian tubes have muscles that contract gently to push an egg toward the uterus; and the tubes are lined with tiny hairlike projections called *cilia*, which also help sweep the egg along toward the uterus. Most often, conception—the joining of an egg and sperm—occurs in the fallopian tubes.

Menstruation—A User's Guide

Understanding your menstrual cycle is vitally important if you want to get the most from almost any method of birth control.

To give the most obvious example, knowing which days of the month you are most likely to conceive is critical to the successful use of natural methods of fertility control. Even users of barrier methods can significantly increase the odds that their method will protect them if they "double up"—using, for example, condoms plus a vaginal spermicide—during the most fertile part of each month.

It is also important for women using hormone-based contraceptives (such as Norplant or birth control pills) to know enough about the normal menstrual cycle so that they understand how and why their cycles are likely to change when they use these methods. For example amenorrhea (no bleeding) can be a normal side effect of Depo-Provera shots and Norplant. But if a woman isn't expecting it and "misses" a period, she might well worry that her method has failed and she is pregnant. Another example: If a woman on oral contraceptives misses a pill or two, where she is in her cycle makes a big difference in how likely it is that her slipup will result in an unplanned pregnancy.

THE CYCLE EXPLAINED

Most women think about their menstrual cycles only in terms of bleeding—when their periods start and stop, how heavy or light, painful or cramp-free they are. This is natural, since bleeding is the only part of the cycle that is visible and tangible. But menstrual bleeding is actually the end result of a month-long chain of events that occurs inside a woman's body.

The whole point of the menstrual cycle—from an evolutionary perspective at least—is to prepare your body for a possible pregnancy. The preparation process itself is an extremely complex sequence that starts in the brain and culminates each month in either (a) pregnancy or (b) menstruation.

There are actually two main events, separate but interrelated, that occur during each menstrual cycle. One is that an egg ripens, or matures, and is released from the ovaries; the other is that the uterine lining thickens and prepares itself to support a pregnancy should that egg become fertilized. If the egg is not fertilized, the uterine lining is shed during menstruation, and the entire sequence of events begins anew.

The first day of bleeding (the visible evidence of the *end* of one menstrual month) is, then, also "day 1" of the *next* month's cycle. At that time *GnRH*, or *gonadotropin-releasing hormone*, a chemical messenger from the hypothalamus (an area of the brain just above the pituitary gland), sends a message to the pituitary to secrete *FSH*, or *follicle-stimulating hormone.* FSH prompts the ovaries to start ripening a number of eggs; and it stimulates the cells surrounding those eggs, called *granulosa cells*, to start to secrete *estrogen.* The estrogen from the granulosa cells stimulates the growth of the lining of the uterus (the endometrium).

By about day 6 of the menstrual cycle, as the follicles continue to develop, one somehow becomes the dominant follicle, the one that will release its mature egg at ovulation. (No one knows how the dominant follicle is "chosen" from the group of eggs that start to ripen at the same time.) As the follicles grow, and more and more estrogen is produced, the rising estrogen levels feed back to the brain, signaling the pituitary to produce less and less FSH.

About midcycle (day 14), the estrogen level peaks, triggering the secretion of *LH,* or *luteinizing hormone,* from the pituitary. LH has several different effects.

First, it causes ovulation, the release of the mature egg from the dominant follicle. After ovulation the egg travels down the fallopian tube to the uterus. If it is not fertilized by a man's sperm within approximately twenty-four hours, the egg will simply dissolve and its components will be reabsorbed by the body. Similarly the other eggs that had started to develop in their follicles will also simply wither away. If that seems like a waste of perfectly good eggs, consider this: A woman is born with about a million eggs in her ovaries. By the time she reaches puberty, about 300,000 viable eggs remain. Since she will need only about 400 to 500 to be released during ovulation in her lifetime, she has plenty of eggs to spare.

Second, LH also causes some of the granulosa cells around the follicles to start producing *progesterone* as well as estrogen. Once the egg has been released, the area where ovulation occurred becomes the *corpus luteum,* and continues to secrete estrogen and progesterone. Progesterone causes the lining of the uterus, now thick from the estrogen stimulation during the first half of the cycle, to change in preparation for the possible implantation of a fertilized egg. The uterine lining, or endometrium, becomes more fluid-filled, and has a higher sugar content for the nourishment of an embryo.

As the cycle continues, more and more progesterone is secreted by the corpus luteum, reaching a peak and plateauing off about eight to ten days after ovulation. Progesterone sends a feedback message to the brain, prompting the pituitary to secrete less LH. If no fertilized egg implants in the uterine lining, progesterone levels fall quickly. Without hormone support the built-up uterine lining sloughs off and menstruation begins.

If, on the other hand, the egg is fertilized and does successfully implant on the uterine wall, the developing *placenta* will take over the job of hormone production from the waning corpus luteum. In that case there will be no decline in hormone levels for the nine months of pregnancy. As long as the hormones remain high, the uterine lining does not shed and no new eggs will start ripening in the ovaries. After the baby is born, hormone levels drop, which is the signal that jump-starts the menstrual cycle into action once again.

Ectopic Pregnancy

An ectopic pregnancy occurs when a fertilized egg implants and starts to grow outside of the uterine cavity. Usually this occurs in one of the fallopian tubes. Very rarely a pregnancy will take hold in the abdomen, outside the uterus.

Ectopics occur, on average, in about one in two hundred pregnancies. They are more common in women who have had a previous ectopic and in those whose tubes have been damaged by infections or, sometimes, endometriosis. To the extent that birth control prevents fertilization, it also reduces the risk of ectopics, compared with women who are not using contraception.

Ectopics can be life-threatening if they are not caught in time. A growing pregnancy can rupture a tube and cause severe internal bleeding. It is important for all sexually active women to know the signs of ectopic pregnancy (a missed period followed by slowly worsening or sudden and severe lower abdominal pain, possibly accompanied by fainting) and seek medical attention promptly. It can sometimes be hard even for doctors to determine the cause of abdominal pain (distinguishing it from appendicitis, for example), but in women of childbearing age ectopic pregnancy should always be a prime suspect. One vital clue: a positive pregnancy test.

If an ectopic is diagnosed very early, it can be treated either surgically or chemically, with a drug called methotrexate. Often, in these cases, the tube can be preserved. Sometimes, especially if there is a delay in the diagnosis, the tube may be so damaged that it must be removed along with the ectopic pregnancy. A woman can go on to have a normal pregnancy after an ectopic, whether she has one tube left or two, although her risk of having another tubal pregnancy is increased.

What About Breastfeeding as Birth Control? Does It Work?

Yes, but . . . Nursing a baby causes the body to produce a hormone called prolactin, which does tend to suppress ovulation. However, only persistent, frequent breastfeeding keeps prolactin levels high enough to prevent egg development—a situation that is most common in cultures where women carry their babies with them during the day and let them suckle at will. In countries such as our own, where nursing mothers are often separated from their infants for hours at a time, breastfeeding as birth control tends to be less reliable. As soon as you start to feed your baby bottles of formula or solid food in addition to breast milk, you will probably start to ovulate again pretty quickly.

Also, if you think about it, you'll realize there's one rather major problem with relying on breastfeeding as birth control: Menstruation is the first visible sign that you're fertile again; but menstruation doesn't occur until *two weeks after you ovulate*. That means that by the time you might have gotten your first period after having had a baby, you could already be pregnant again.

When During the Menstrual Cycle Is Unprotected Sex "Safe"?

The sequence of events described above means that a typical woman can conceive from the day an egg is released (which happens about two weeks after the first day of your last period) until a day or so later, when that egg dissolves and can no longer be fertilized.

But you also must take into account the fact that sperm can live in a woman's reproductive tract for several days. Three days is perhaps typical, but studies have shown sperm survival for as long as a week. That means unprotected sex in the days *before* ovulation can also result in a pregnancy.

And add to that the fact that very few women have absolutely regular, "classic" twenty-eight-day cycles, and you start to see why it can be hard to figure out when it might truly be "safe" to have sex without birth control. (The ways in which natural methods of birth control attempt to predict "safe" times will be discussed in detail in chapter 4. Suffice it to say here that unpredictable variations in menstrual cycles and sperm survival are one reason this approach to birth control tends to have high failure rates. In order to work, natural methods need consistent use by couples who are committed to making them work.)

Menstrual cycles also don't stay the same over a woman's reproductive lifetime. For the first few months after menarche (the onset of menstruation, which occurs typically at about age eleven or twelve) periods tend to be irregular and unpredictable. The middle years of fertility (from about age eighteen to thirty-five) tend to have the most regular menstrual cycles, although even then they can be thrown off by such common occurrences as stress, illness, or significant weight gain or loss. Later in the reproductive years, after about age thirty-five or so, a slow decline in fertility can again cause menstrual-cycle shifts. At first these are likely to be as subtle as a slight shortening of the cycle, by perhaps a day or two. Later, after age forty, women tend to get more irregular and start skipping periods occasionally and unpredictably.

3

TALKING TO YOUR DOCTOR ABOUT BIRTH CONTROL

Think of your doctor as a partner in your quest for the best possible method of birth control.

For the best results, the more you give—information-wise—the more you'll get. Your health care provider (he or she could be a private or HMO ob/gyn, a family practitioner, a college health service physician, or a counselor at a family planning clinic) may know a lot about human reproduction and contraception *in general*, but he or she doesn't know a thing about *you* as an individual. So the more background information you can give your doctor, and the more open and honest you can be, the more likely it is that you will end up with a method that suits your lifestyle and your personality, as well as your physical needs.

Also the more you know about birth control before you walk into your doctor's office, the more you can learn from him or her. These days almost no health professional has the time he or she might wish to spend educating women about every aspect of each method. If you come prepared, more time can be spent on your specific questions and concerns, and less on covering the basics.

Making It Easier to Talk

The things you need to discuss with your doctor are very personal, and therefore can be a bit awkward to talk about. To make opening up a bit easier, keep the following points in mind:

■ No matter how complicated or unusual your circumstances, you're not likely to shock or surprise your doctor. He or she has almost certainly heard anything you have to say—and probably a lot worse—before. Remind yourself that your doctor is there to help, not to judge.

■ Don't worry about terminology. You don't have to speak in technical or medical terms for your doctor to understand your concerns. Just use whatever words are comfortable, and be as clear and complete as possible.

■ Anything that's important to *you* should be taken seriously by your health care provider. If you're concerned about the possibility of weight gain or acne if you go on the Pill, say so. If your boyfriend absolutely despises condoms, don't agree to use them when you know you really won't. If your current doctor recommends a diaphragm, and a past doctor told you you couldn't use one because of your tipped uterus, speak up and ask where the discrepancy comes from.

■ Don't hesitate to ask for an explanation of any technical terms that aren't absolutely clear to you. Your doctor is not going to think you're stupid; he or she knows you don't have a medical degree. Medical lingo is so familiar to health workers that half the time they probably don't even realize they're speaking what sounds like a foreign language to the rest of us.

■ And a final, very important point: Everything you tell your doctor—everything that goes in your medical records—is confidential. You don't have to worry about revealing such facts as, for example, a past abortion or a bout with a sexually transmitted disease that you've never even told your parents or your boyfriend or your husband about.

What Your Doctor Needs to Know About You

Many facets of your health history, both current and past, enter into the birth control decision. The following are some of the things your doctor will want to know about you to help you zero in on the best possible contraceptive method. As you read about them, you might want to jot down things that come to mind about your own health and medical history. Also write down any questions you may have for your doctor. That way you can take your notes with you to your appointment and have the information at your fingertips. By being prepared ahead of time, you can relax and concentrate on talking with your doctor instead of listening with half your attention while the other half is struggling not to forget when your last period started.

■ *Menstrual cycle.* The date of your last period is just one of many things your health care provider will need to know about your menstrual cycle in order to help you choose an appropriate contraceptive. If your cycles are erratic and irregular, for example, fertility awareness methods may be almost impossible to use successfully. If your periods include heavy bleeding and severe cramping, the IUD is probably not a good choice because it can make those symptoms worse. The Pill, on the other hand, often brings about a lighter flow, fewer days of bleeding, and less cramping.

■ *Fertility.* Have you ever been pregnant? If you have, were you trying to get pregnant, or trying not to (i.e., were you using birth control at the time)? If you got pregnant because of a birth control failure, do you know what went wrong, or were you using the method perfectly, as far as you know?

How important is it that you not get pregnant at this point in your life? Would an accidental pregnancy derail your college plans? Are you married and planning on having a family, just not quite yet? Are you very sure the three kids you have are enough, or would another sort-of-unplanned pregnancy not really be a big deal? Are you thirty-five and not yet married and extremely concerned about preserving your fertility for as long as possible? Each of these situations has very different implications when it comes to your birth control choice. And if your doctor understands where you're coming from, you are much more likely to end up with a contraceptive that will work well at this stage of your life—whatever that stage may be.

Age is a very important factor when it comes to choosing a birth control method, and it's one that probably isn't considered as much as it should be. For young, highly fertile women there is less margin for error in a birth control method. If you misuse or don't use contraception at this point in your life, or if you use a method that has a high failure rate even if it is used correctly, you may be quite likely to get pregnant. Older women, on the other hand, may be able to successfully "get away with" a contraceptive that's a bit less effective, such as a diaphragm or cervical cap, because they are somewhat less fertile.

▪ *Past birth control use.* Your doctor is going to want to know what methods you have used in the past, and why you stopped using them. Did you go off the Pill because you had breakthrough bleeding? If so, there's a good chance that a different formulation might not have the same side effects. Or did you stop because you broke up with your longtime boyfriend and didn't want to take medication every day when you knew you weren't going to be having sex with anyone for a while? Is there a particular method that interests you now that you want to ask the doctor about?

▪ *Your current sex life.* Are you married, single, divorced? Just now preparing for your first sexual relationship? Are you in a long-standing one-man-only relationship, or are you at a point in your life where you might have more than one partner? (This last includes "serial monogamy"—where a woman has sex only with her boyfriend, but over time has a number of sequential relationships.)

These questions are important because of the risk of sexually transmitted diseases. Some birth control methods (particularly condoms, both male and female) offer very good protection from most STDs, including HIV, the virus that causes AIDS. Diaphragms and cervical caps provide less protection, the IUD none whatsoever. Hormonal methods, such as the Pill, Norplant, and Depo-Provera, don't keep women from catching infections, but because they make the cervical mucus thick and less penetrable, they may reduce the risk that germs will travel up through the cervix and possibly cause a tubal or pelvic infection. To protect themselves from infections, many women these days use condoms with new partners in addition to the pills they take for protection against accidental pregnancy.

Your current situation is also relevant in terms of the availability of your method. To work, your method has to be where you are when you need it. One of the major reasons for un-intended pregnancies among birth control users is that their method either wasn't available or wasn't used when they had sex. Take, for example, a college student who sometimes has sex with her boyfriend in her dorm room and other times sleeps over at his apartment. A stash of condoms and spermi-cide in both places might be an excellent option (and one that protects against both pregnancy and STDs when used every time you have sex). Birth control pills or a diaphragm are trickier. These methods will only work if she trains herself to carry them in the backpack that goes everywhere with her, in-stead of leaving them at home in her bedside table or bath-room cabinet.

■ *Health conditions.* It is very important that your doctor know about any medical conditions you have or medications you take, since these can affect your choice of a birth control method.

Medical conditions are probably most relevant when it comes to hormonal methods, such as the Pill, Depo-Provera, and Norplant. For example, if you have a history of throm-bophlebitis (blood clots and/or inflammation in the veins), breast cancer, or some types of liver diseases, these methods will probably not be an option. If you have uncontrolled high blood pressure or elevated cholesterol, the Pill may not be your best choice. Dilantin, taken to control epilepsy, can in-teract with oral contraceptives to make them less effective. On the other hand if you have endometriosis, it might actu-ally get better if you take oral contraceptives. And if you are a young woman with a strong family history of ovarian cancer, a doctor might encourage Pill use, since it has been shown to significantly reduce the risk of this deadly disease.

There are also medical conditions that can affect your choice of nonhormonal contraceptives. If you take steroids, an IUD is not a good choice. This method would also most likely not be an option for women who have had PID (pelvic inflammatory disease, a serious infection that can cause infertility).

Are you bothered by recurrent cystitis? In some women diaphragms can make this problem worse. Have you had cervical problems, abnormal Pap smears? If so, a cervical cap might not be the best choice for you. Diaphragms and condoms and female condoms may, on the other hand, actually protect you against cervical cancer, since many experts feel this disease is linked to the sexual transmission of a virus called HPV, human papillomavirus. Are you allergic to latex? That's what condoms and diaphragms are made of. Do you have fibroids (noncancerous tumors of the uterus)? You can probably use an IUD as long as the uterine cavity is not misshapen by them. The Pill wouldn't have been an option years ago, when higher doses of estrogen sometimes caused fibroids to grow, but with today's low-dose formulations, this is no longer a problem.

Take Information Home to Read

Ask for any written information your doctor may have about the methods you're considering, or the method you have chosen. Be sure to read everything carefully, and call your doctor right away if you come across anything that makes you think you shouldn't use that contraceptive after all. No matter how carefully you and your doctor try to go over the relevant ground, sometimes things get missed, or misunderstood. Nobody's perfect. And realistically there's simply not time for every doctor to ask every patient every possible question. (See "What You Should Leave Your Doctor's Office Knowing," page 46.)

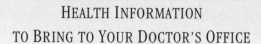

HEALTH INFORMATION
TO BRING TO YOUR DOCTOR'S OFFICE

To help your doctor help you zero in on the best birth control method, write down the answers to the following questions (or at least think about them beforehand):

- MENSTRUAL CYCLE
  When did your last period start?
  How long did bleeding last?
  How heavy was the bleeding?
  Did you have cramps? Did you take anything for them?
  How old were you when your periods started?
  Are your cycles regular or irregular?

- PAST BIRTH CONTROL USE
  What methods have you used in the past?
  Why did you stop using them?
  What did you like and dislike about them?

- FERTILITY
  Have you ever been pregnant?
  Have you ever carried a baby to term?
  Have you had a miscarriage?
  Have you had an abortion?

- GENERAL HEALTH
  How old are you?
  Do you take any doctor-prescribed medication?
  Do you regularly take any over-the-counter medication?
  Do you have any medical conditions or health problems?

You also need to study any information you can get about how to use the method correctly. Call if there's anything you don't understand: It's better to be a bit of a pest than to make a mistake that leaves you at risk for an unintended pregnancy. Often a nurse or physician's assistant in your doctor's office can also answer questions.

WHAT YOU SHOULD LEAVE YOUR DOCTOR'S OFFICE KNOWING

Before you leave the doctor's office—having chosen a contraceptive method—be sure that you know the following:

- How to use your birth control correctly
- What your chances are of getting pregnant while using it
- What to do if you mess up—if you forget to take your pill before you go to bed, for example
- What the possible side effects are, and which ones you need to report to your doctor
- What is the best time of day to call the doctor's office with questions that come up after your appointment
- Who, besides your doctor, can answer your questions

Part Two

❧

"NATURAL" BIRTH CONTROL

FERTILITY AWARENESS METHODS

Currently Available

Ovulation Method
Temperature Tracking
Sympto-Thermal Techniques
Rhythm

Fertility awareness methods may also be known as natural family planning and are sometimes more technically referred to as sympto-thermal techniques. Some of the most commonly used approaches to natural fertility control include charting the days of the menstrual cycle, daily temperature taking, and the observation of changes in cervical mucus. The cervical mucus technique is sometimes called the ovulation method or the Billings method. You may also have heard of the rhythm or calendar method, a term that generally refers to counting days in the menstrual cycle. These days rhythm alone is not considered by many proponents of natural methods to be an effective means of natural family planning.

It is hard to estimate with much scientific accuracy how

many women rely on fertility awareness methods, either alone or in conjunction with other forms of birth control. The Ortho 1995 Annual Birth Control Study puts 9 percent of women in the categories they called rhythm and withdrawal. The 1988 National Survey of Family Growth found that about 4 percent of women said they used some type of fertility awareness; about a third of those women said they also used another form of birth control as well.

What It Is

All fertility awareness methods involve daily observation of various changes in the female body that indicate the approach of ovulation, so that intercourse can be avoided during the days of the month when a woman is most likely to get pregnant. Note: Although they may sound simple, you should not try these methods until you attend a class or get individual instruction in their use from a family planning counselor.

The same fertility awareness techniques can also be used to increase your chances of conception when you *do* want to have a baby.

How It Works

At different times during the menstrual cycle certain relatively predictable changes occur that, if carefully followed, can alert couples that it's time to avoid sex if they don't want to risk conception.

CERVICAL MUCUS METHOD. During fertile times of the month the cervical mucus becomes more copious and may be seen and felt as a liquid discharge from the vagina. This clear, slippery-feeling fluid (which at times can be stretched from thumb to finger) helps to nourish sperm and is a consistency that helps the sperm make their way up the reproductive tract to the egg. Even if you can't actually see any mucus during your fertile days, your vaginal opening and lips may feel slightly wet or slippery.

To keep tabs on your cervical mucus, you have to get into the habit of checking at least once a day (even every time you go to the bathroom). See if you can collect any discharge from the vaginal opening on a finger or some toilet paper. Note how much there is, if any, and its consistency.

During the time of month that a woman is *not* fertile, the cervical mucus tends to be scant, stickier, and less "stretchable." It is more likely to stay in or near the cervix, serving as a physical barrier that is hard for sperm to penetrate. During this nonfertile time you may feel "dryer" and have no visible vaginal discharge. These descriptions are general: your cervical mucus, and the changes it goes through may be different, since there is quite a bit of normal variation from woman to woman.

To be safest, all penis-to-vagina contact should be avoided (or, if you want to have sex, use a contraceptive) when the "fertile" mucus is present—and for several days after it is no longer detectable. Ovulation usually occurs around the time of month that the "fertile" mucus stops being produced (within a day or two before or after). The egg only lives for about a day if it is not fertilized, but sperm have been shown to live for as long as a week in the female reproductive tract (although they probably more typically survive about three days). Therefore some instructors advise avoiding sex as soon as any of the fertile-type cervical mucus (or a wet feeling) appears. Because menstrual blood could obscure the very early changes in the cervical mucus, especially if you have long periods, you may also be advised that it's not absolutely safe to have sex during your period.

Some vaginal infections, including yeast and sexually transmitted diseases such as trichomoniasis, can cause a vaginal discharge. It can be hard for someone without medical training to distinguish these abnormal types of discharge from the normal changes in cervical mucus.

There are also normal and natural discharges from the vagina during and after sex that can make it more difficult to distinguish cyclical changes in the cervical mucus. For this reason some proponents of this method recommend that you only have sex every other day after your period ends, on the theory that this will make it easier to distinguish sex-related discharges from cervical mucus.

TEMPERATURE METHOD. Your temperature when you first wake up in the morning, before you get out of bed (or do anything active in bed), is known as your basal temperature. Generally your basal temperature will go up and down at certain predictable times during the menstrual cycle.

In order to use basal temperature as an indicator of fertility, you take your temperature first thing every morning and mark the result on a chart. (A special "basal" thermometer can make it easier to detect the relatively small cyclical changes in temperature.) Normally your temperature will drop slightly just before ovulation, then rise a half degree or more for several days in a row afterward. Your temperature will probably stay elevated until your period begins, then it will fall to the original level and stay there until it drops again just before ovulation the next month. If your temperature doesn't rise, you may not have ovulated that month. If your temperature remains elevated and bleeding does not occur, you may be pregnant. Because of individual variations, it can take several menstrual cycles before you get the hang of what your cycle tends to look like on a temperature chart. As you can see on the sample basal temperature–tracking chart on the opposite page, this isn't a matter of straight, simple ups and downs.

BASAL TEMPERATURE AND MUCUS CHART

MONTH *April* thru *May*

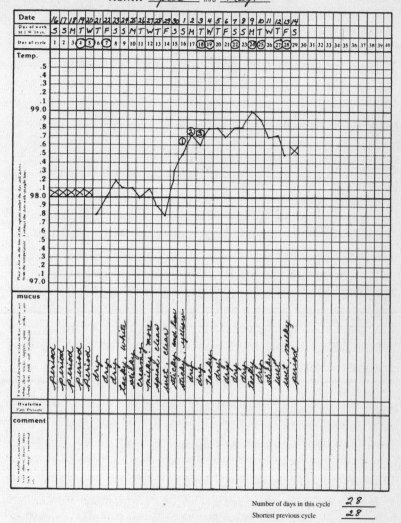

Number of days in this cycle *28*

Shortest previous cycle *28*

(Reprinted by permission from Margaret Nofziger, A Cooperative Method of Natural Birth Control, © 1992. Book Publishing Company.)

SAMPLE BASAL TEMPERATURE AND CERVICAL MUCUS CHART

One important limitation of temperature charting is that it cannot always predict ovulation far enough in advance. If, for example, you happen to have sex the night *before* your temperature drops, live sperm could still be in the uterus and tubes when you ovulate a day or so later, and be able to fertilize the egg. Also your basal temperature can be thrown off its usual course by a number of life's common disruptions, including illness, lack of sleep, stress, and travel.

SYMPTO-THERMAL TECHNIQUES. Women using what is sometimes referred to as the sympto-thermal method may be taught to use some combination of the above strategies and learn to note, as well, additional menstrual cycle "symptoms," such as the midcycle pain that can occur with ovulation and the breast tenderness that often precedes menstruation. Using different approaches together can increase the effectiveness of natural family planning—and can also add up to quite a bit of record keeping. Some women find all the tracking and charting cumbersome; for others it soon becomes a familiar part of the daily routine, and a reasonable trade-off for drug- and device-free contraception.

RHYTHM. Typically the rhythm or calendar method depends on abstaining from sex during a woman's probable fertile days based only on counting the days of the menstrual cycle. Typically ovulation occurs on day 14, plus or minus a day or two, from the onset of your last period. (More precisely it occurs about fourteen days *before* your next period starts.) The egg, once released, lives about one day. Sperm, as we've noted, can generally survive for about three days in the female reproductive tract.

Therefore if all goes according to schedule, you should be able to avoid conception if you don't have sex from about day 9 (counting backward two days from day 14, in case ovulation comes early, then three more to compensate for sperm's life span) to about day 16 (day 14 plus two in case of late ovulation). Unprotected sex would of course be most risky right around midcycle.

One of the significant limitations of rhythm is that many women have irregular cycles, and most have them at least some of the time. This method works best if you chart several menstrual cycles before you start to rely on rhythm for contraception, so that you get an idea of how long and how regular your periods tend to be.

WITHDRAWAL. Withdrawal, also called coitus interruptus, involves removing the penis from the vagina before the man ejaculates. It is not considered to be an effective contraceptive by many proponents of natural family planning.

Probably the biggest problem with withdrawal is that it takes extreme (some might say superhuman) control for a man to pull out of the vagina while on the verge of a climax. It may be hard for the young or sexually inexperienced to know when ejaculation is impending. Having to remove the penis before orgasm may make sex less enjoyable, for one or both partners. Even if the man does remove his penis in time, he may not get far enough away, and sperm may fall on his partner's external genitals and thereby gain access to her vagina. In addition there is the possibility that there could be sperm in the pre-ejaculate (drops of fluid that are discharged from the penis before a man comes), particularly if you have sex more than once within a few hours. The chance of pregnancy from pre-ejaculate is probably quite low, but theoretically it could happen.

How Effective It Is

It's hard to know exactly how many women get pregnant while using fertility awareness methods, for a number of reasons. For one thing, as you have seen, this method isn't a single means of birth control, but several different techniques—which can be used alone or in combination. (Some people also combine fertility awareness techniques with other types of birth control, such as condoms, during fertile days.) Also the effectiveness of the "natural" techniques depends both on how carefully and consistently a couple uses them and, perhaps even more importantly, on *how consistently they abstain from sex when they know they're likely to conceive.*

And finally, there are simply not as many well-done scientific studies on most of these methods as there are for contraceptives such as birth control pills. There was one recent study, published in the *New England Journal of Medicine*, that looked at exactly when during the menstrual cycle sex was most likely to result in a pregnancy. Interestingly, virtually all conceptions occurred when couples had sex during the five days *before* ovulation, or on the estimated day of ovulation itself. After ovulation occurred the chances of pregnancy were remote.

From the numbers that are available it is clear that effectiveness varies widely. On average, however, those who depend on fertility awareness methods tend to have relatively high pregnancy rates: Typically, according to *Contraceptive Technology*, about twenty women out of one hundred will get pregnant in a year, not much higher than the eighteen per one hundred who might get pregnant using a diaphragm. If you are young and fertile and tend to have sex frequently, your risk may be higher. And if one hundred women were to use one or a combination of natural methods to the absolute best of their ability for one year, the pregnancy rate could range from as low as 1 percent to about 9 percent. Realistically, however, such low pregnancy rates could be expected only from the most highly motivated and consistently careful of couples.

How Much It Costs

These methods cost next to nothing to use. Basal thermometers (which are sensitive to very small changes in body temperature) are widely available at pharmacies for about ten dollars.

The Advantages of This Method

Fertility control methods can be used by couples who, for religious or personal reasons, wish to avoid "artificial" forms of birth control.

These methods do not involve the use of any drugs or devices (except, if you chart your temperature, a thermometer).

These methods do not affect a woman's menstrual cycle or hormones.

Fertility awareness techniques can be used along with other methods—such as barrier contraceptives like condoms and diaphragms—to further decrease the risk of unplanned pregnancy.

The techniques of fertility awareness can also help couples recognize their most fertile times, so they can more easily conceive a child when they want to.

Learning these methods can help women become generally more knowledgeable about and comfortable with their bodies and their menstrual cycles.

The Disadvantages of This Method

It takes motivation, record keeping, and attention to detail to successfully practice the techniques of natural family planning.

It can take several months of charting the body's natural fluctuations (temperature, cervical mucus, or a combination of the two) before most women can use these methods with confidence.

It can be hard to observe the changes in cervical mucus accurately. It can be difficult for someone who is not a trained professional to distinguish normal cervical mucus from some types of vaginal infections. In addition, changes in the cervical mucus may be obscured by the vaginal discharge that occurs during and after sex, and also by menstrual blood.

These methods can interfere with the spontaneity of sex. It takes self-control for couples to avoid having sex during fertile times of the month. Intercourse must be avoided for a significant portion of each month for these methods to be most effective. (Exactly how long depends largely on your cycle's length and regularity.)

These methods provide no protection against sexually transmitted diseases—which include everything from the very common herpes and chlamydia to HIV, the incurable virus that causes AIDS.

Reversibility

All natural methods are immediately and completely reversible. As we have said, many of the same strategies that are useful in helping couples avoid pregnancy can also be used to help them conceive when they are ready to have a child.

Safety and Side Effects

Natural family planning techniques have no direct side effects and are often described as being entirely safe. However, one "risk" that women should consider carefully if they decide to use this approach is that the risk of unplanned pregnancy is higher than with many other methods.

Who Is a Good Candidate for This Method

Couples who cannot or choose not to use any other type of birth control.

Women with regular, predictable periods.

Women who are willing and able consistently to carry out the self-testing necessary to zero in on the time of ovulation.

Couples who have a high level of self-control.

Couples who have sex relatively infrequently (once or twice a month, for example), since they may find it less of a problem to adapt to timed periods of abstinence.

Women over forty, whose fertility is lower, as long as their periods are still regular and predictable.

Who Is Not a Good Candidate for This Method

Women with irregular, unpredictable periods (which can be a sign that ovulation is also irregular and unpredictable) may find it difficult to use these techniques with confidence.

Young, highly fertile women, since they are more likely to have failures with this method, particularly if they have sex frequently (more than twice a week), which increases the odds that there will be live sperm in their reproductive tracts at the time of ovulation.

Couples who find it hard to refrain from vaginal intercourse during "unsafe" times of the month.

NOTE: To work best, fertility awareness techniques require counseling. *Don't try to figure them out on your own, or put them to practice after simply reading about them here.* For more information:

■ A local family planning clinic (such as Planned Parenthood) may have written information and counselors who can help women learn how to monitor their cyclic changes.

■ Many hospitals (particularly Catholic hospitals) have information available or hold classes to teach the techniques of fertility awareness.

■ Contact Family of the Americas for information about the ovulation method. (See appendix for their address and phone number.)

■ Look for books devoted to this topic at a library or bookstore. (See appendix for one example.)

■ Talk to your doctor.

Part Three

❧

BARRIER
METHODS

CHAPTER

5
___

CONDOMS

Currently Available

Dozens of types of condoms are widely available without a prescription at pharmacies, convenience stores, supermarkets, and so on. Common brand names include Ramses, Lady Protex, and Sheik (all from Schmid); Lifestyles (Ansell); Saxon and Circle Coin (Safetex); Trojan (Carter-Wallace). Condoms come in a variety of shapes, surface textures, and colors, lubricated and nonlubricated, with and without spermicide.

According to the Ortho 1995 Annual Birth Control Study the condom is now the third most popular form of birth control in this country, ranking just below sterilization and the Pill. Currently about 19 percent of women age fifteen to fifty report that their partners use condoms. More than one in three (34 percent) young, unmarried women reported condom use. Almost half (46 percent) use condoms along with another method (such as the Pill) to protect themselves against sexually transmitted diseases, particularly HIV, the virus that causes AIDS.

What It Is

A thin, stretchy sheath about two inches wide and six inches long, designed to be worn over the penis during sex. Condoms form a physical barrier between penis and vagina and also hold sperm after ejaculation so that it cannot travel into the woman's reproductive tract to fertilize an egg.

The vast majority of condoms are made of latex, a form of natural rubber. Condoms made of lamb intestine are often referred to as skin or natural-membrane condoms. There is also one new brand (Avanti, Schmid Laboratories; FDA approved in 1994) of condom that is made of polyurethane, the same material as the female condom.

How It Works

Condoms come rolled up, in small individual packets. To use one, unroll it (being sure you have it right side out, so that it unrolls easily) onto the man's penis after he has an erection. The condom should reach all the way down to the base of the penis near the man's pubic hair. It must be put on before the penis has *any* contact with the woman's genital area. It is possible that the small amount of fluid that comes out of the penis before ejaculation (climax) could contain sperm, particularly if you have sex more than once within a short period of time. If the condom has a plain tip instead of a reservoir tip, squeeze out the air and leave about a half inch at the head of the penis to hold the semen. If the man has not been circumcised, the foreskin should be pulled back to put the condom on.

The penis should be withdrawn from the vagina as soon as the man ejaculates (reaches his climax or comes), before the penis starts to soften. The condom should be held close to the base of the penis while this is done. Once the penis is well

BEFORE SEX
Use a new condom every time you have sex—before foreplay, before penis gets anywhere near any body opening. (To avoid exposure to any body fluid that can carry infection.) Handle condom gently.

Put condom on as soon as penis is hard. Be sure rolled-up ring is on the outside. And leave space at tip to hold semen when you come.

Squeeze tip gently so no air is trapped inside. Hold tip while you unroll condom . . . all the way down to the hair. If condom doesn't unroll, it's on wrong. Throw it away. Start over with a new one.

("Using condoms" reprinted with permission of Planned Parenthood of New York City, Inc.)

PUTTING ON A CONDOM

away from the woman's genitals, the condom should be taken off carefully, without spilling any of the semen.

Condoms are designed to be used once, then thrown away. If you have sex again, no matter how soon, you should use a new condom. If you put a condom on the tip of the penis to unroll it, and discover it is inside out, you should throw that one away and use another one. Wrap used condoms in toilet paper or facial tissue before you throw them away so that no one else will end up touching the secretions. (Many people flush used condoms down the toilet, but it's not good for the sewage system.)

How Effective It Is

Used correctly, condoms are a very effective method of birth control. If latex condoms were used exactly according to directions every time a couple had sex, the failure rate would probably be as low as 3 percent—surprisingly close to that of the Pill. Average pregnancy rates are significantly higher: Out of one hundred typical users, about twelve will get pregnant. That's a bit more effective than the diaphragm, quite a bit less effective than the Pill, and vastly more effective than no method at all; 85 percent of couples who use no type of contraception can expect to get pregnant in a year.

Using a condom plus a vaginal spermicide increases its effectiveness. There is not good scientific evidence to show whether condoms that come with spermicide already on them work any better at preventing pregnancy or sexually transmitted diseases than plain condoms.

About 12 million people in this country are infected with a sexually transmitted disease each year. Two-thirds of AIDS victims got the disease from having sex with an infected partner. Latex condoms provide more protection against sexually transmitted diseases (particularly HIV, the virus that causes AIDS) than any other birth control method. The only thing safer than condoms is abstaining from sex altogether. (Mutual monogamy is also safe *if you can be sure that both you and your partner are disease-free.*) For STD protection condoms can be used during anal and oral sex, as well as for vaginal intercourse.

Condoms also provide significant protection against other STDs besides HIV. They are quite good at preventing the transmission of human papillomavirus (HPV) from the penis to the cervix. This extremely common infection causes genital warts and has been linked to cervical cancer. Condoms also provide significant protection against chlamydia and gonorrhea. Condoms are less good at preventing the spread of herpes, since this infection is spread by skin-to-skin contact, and lesions (sores) can appear on body parts not shielded by a condom (such as the buttocks, the vulva in a woman, or the scrotum in a man).

Lamb-intestine condoms have microscopic pores, smaller than sperm, but big enough to let some disease-causing germs through, and should not be used for protection against STDs. Laboratory tests on polyurethane condoms (both male and female) suggest that this material should be very good at blocking diseases, but so far there is limited information about how well it works with real people under normal circumstances.

How Much It Costs

Latex condoms generally cost about fifty cents each or less, making this one of the most inexpensive contraceptives available. If you have sex twice a week for a year, it would add up to about one hundred dollars. Sheep-intestine and polyurethane condoms cost more. If you get latex condoms from a family planning clinic or college health service, they may cost even less.

The Advantages of This Method

Condoms are widely available and don't require a prescription.

Condoms are relatively inexpensive, and you only need to buy them when you need them. (In contrast, for example, you have to take the Pill every day, even if you have sex only on

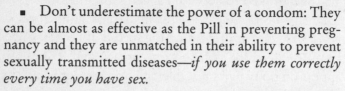

TIPS FOR SUCCESSFUL CONDOM USE

■ Don't underestimate the power of a condom: They can be almost as effective as the Pill in preventing pregnancy and they are unmatched in their ability to prevent sexually transmitted diseases—*if you use them correctly every time you have sex.*

■ For an extra edge of protection, against both pregnancy and diseases, use a vaginal spermicide along with condoms. You can put a little bit in the tip of the condom before you put it on, and a little more on the outside of the condom after you put it on—or use an applicator to put extra spermicide directly into the vagina.

■ Be sure the condoms you buy say on the label that they provide protection against sexually transmitted diseases. Not all condoms do (lambskin, some imported condoms), and only those that do can say so on the label.

■ Put the condom on before there is any contact between penis and vagina. A small amount of fluid (possibly containing enough sperm to cause a pregnancy) comes out of the penis before ejaculation.

■ For the most complete protection against STDs, use condoms during oral and anal sex, as well as for vaginal intercourse. (Condoms may be more likely to break during anal sex.) If you're going to have oral sex, apply spermicide afterward. It won't hurt you but it doesn't taste good.

■ Use a new condom every time. Don't try to reuse them.

■ Don't use Vaseline, baby oil, skin creams or any type of oil-containing products for extra lubrication, since they can weaken latex. There are a number of condom-safe lubricants available. (K-Y jelly is one popular brand.) Spermicides also work for lubrication.

■ Condoms vary in length and width, in how lubricated they are (how "slippery" they feel), in surface texture (ribbed, studded, etc.), color, flavor, and more. If you or your partner don't like one kind, try others until you find one you like better.

■ If the condom is too tight, it may be more likely to break; if it's too loose, it may slip off during sex.

■ Keep extra condoms away from heat and light (pockets, car glove compartments, and wallets are not recommended). Open the packet just before you use it, and toss any condom that's not soft, flexible, and fresh-looking.

■ Be careful not to snag the condom on long fingernails, teeth, or jewelry.

■ If a condom breaks or comes off during sex, wash with soap and water right away (which can reduce the risk of infection, not pregnancy). It is sometimes recommended that a woman immediately apply a vaginal spermicide in this situation. While this may reduce the number of live sperm in her reproductive tract, sperm swim fast, and some are likely to get through the cervix before you can get the spermicide in place. (Another good reason to use condoms plus spermicide to begin with.) You may want to call your doctor or clinic for advice if the breakage or slip-off occurs around midcycle, when you would be likely to be ovulating. Depending on a number of factors (such as your medical history and exactly when during sex the condom actually broke), you might be a candidate for the "morning-after" pill. (See chapter 17, "When Birth Control Fails.") If so, it must be taken within seventy-two hours.

weekends; and methods such as IUDs and Norplant must be paid for up front and remain active in your body whether you need contraceptive protection or not.)

Condoms can be used along with other types of contraceptives (such as the Pill or an IUD) specifically for disease protection.

Condoms are a good backup to have on hand for added contraceptive protection in case you forget to take a birth control pill.

The Disadvantages of This Method

For condoms to work, you have to use them every time you have sex.

Unlike other barrier methods, this is not a contraceptive women can use to protect themselves: The man must be a willing and active participant.

It takes discipline to use condoms correctly. You have to put them on during sex—after a man has an erection— and take them off again while the penis is still hard after ejaculation.

Some people find it embarrassing to buy condoms at a store, or to talk about using them with a new sexual partner.

Men frequently complain that they don't like the way condoms feel—that they don't transmit body warmth, for example, and that they cut down on sensation. Then again, millions of couples have found ways to enjoy sex with condoms in spite of these limitations. And as more and more women start to insist on condom use to protect themselves from STDs, more and more men are likely to decide that sex with a condom beats no sex at all.

Reversibility

Condoms are immediately and completely reversible: Any time you don't use one, you could get pregnant.

Safety and Side Effects

Condoms are very safe and have virtually no side effects. They don't affect sperm production or the semen itself in a man or the menstrual cycle or hormone levels in a woman.

A small number of people are allergic to latex and will be unable to use condoms (or diaphragms or cervical caps) made out of this material. For them a polyurethane condom (male or female) might be a good alternative.

Who Is a Good Candidate for This Method

Women whose partners are willing to use condoms.

Couples with good self-control and the discipline to use condoms every time they have sex.

People who are at risk for sexually transmitted diseases.

Who Is Not a Good Candidate for This Method

Women whose partners won't use condoms.

People who are sensitive to latex.

6

FEMALE
CONDOMS

Currently Available

Reality female condom (Female Health Company, Wisconsin Pharmacal). The female condom was approved by the FDA in 1993 and has been widely available in this country since 1994. Because this method is still relatively new, we are unable to reliably report how many women are using it.

What It Is

A thin, colorless, flexible tube of polyurethane, about 6 inches long and 2 inches wide, that is open at one end and closed at the other. There are rings at each end, both of which are softer, thinner, and more flexible than the ring that forms the rim of a diaphragm. The female condom is designed to be worn by the woman, lining the vagina. This method is intended to provide protection against both pregnancy and sexually transmitted diseases. Unlike a diaphragm, the female condom is used alone, without additional spermicide; also unlike a diaphragm, the female condom is "one size fits all."

How It Works

The female condom is a physical barrier between a woman's vagina and a man's penis. It catches and holds the semen that is released from the penis so that the sperm cannot enter the woman's reproductive tract and fertilize an egg.

Female condoms, like their male counterparts, are available without a prescription at drugstores, supermarkets, and so on. They come individually wrapped in plastic pouches that are bigger than the tiny packets that hold male condoms, since Reality does not come rolled up like a male condom. Like male condoms, female condoms are designed to be used one time only, then thrown away.

The female condom looks like a stretched-out version of male condoms, except for the soft rings at each end, which help hold it in place. The inner ring is held close to the cervix by the pubic bone, the way a diaphragm is; the outer ring simply rests outside the body, covering the vaginal lips (the labia).

You can put in the female condom standing up, squatting, or lying down. Although technically it can be inserted as long as eight hours ahead of time, according to the package insert, most women will probably find it more comfortable to insert the condom just before they have sex, instead of walking around with it in. Wash your hands before inserting the female condom. To put it in, hold the vaginal lips apart with one hand, and use the other hand to squeeze the inner ring flat and slide the condom into the vagina. Be sure you put the *closed* end (with the smaller ring) into the vagina. Keep pushing the inner ring with your finger until it is all the way up the vagina, past the pubic bone. When it's in right, the inner ring will be hooked behind your pubic bone and the outer ring will be lying against your vaginal lips on your pubic hair. (About

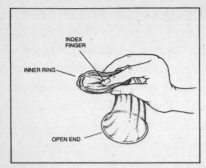

1. Inner ring is squeezed for insertion

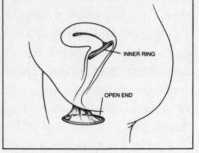

2. Sheath is inserted, similarly to a tampon

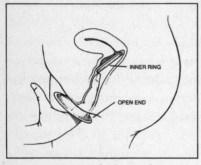

3. Inner ring is pushed up as far as it can go with index finger

4. In place

(Courtesy of The Female Health Company)

INSERTING THE FEMALE CONDOM

an inch of the tube will usually be visible, too.) The condom must lie straight, not twisted, in the vagina.

After the man ejaculates, pinch the outer ring closed and twist the condom to keep the semen inside. Then gently pull the condom out, wrap it in tissues or toilet paper, and throw it away. Don't flush it down the toilet (it's bad for the sewage system), and don't try to wash it out and use it again. If you have sex again, you need to use a new condom.

While you don't have to take the female condom out immediately after the man ejaculates, as you do with a male condom, it is still a good idea to remove it relatively quickly, and definitely before you stand up—so semen doesn't leak. (The reason the penis and male condom have to be withdrawn *immediately* is that the condom won't fit tightly as the penis softens, and semen could seep out.)

How Effective It Is

In the six-month clinical trials of the female condom, pregnancy rates were about 13 percent, which—doubled—would make the annual pregnancy rate about 26 percent. Those are the statistics you will see on the package insert (and is a higher pregnancy rate than is typically cited for male condoms or diaphragms), but some experts think female condoms actually work better than this number suggests. Failures tend to taper off after people have used a method for a while and gotten the hang of it, so accidental pregnancies in the second six months should be lower than during the first six months (bringing the yearly total down). But because female condoms have not been around that long, and because studies on other barrier methods were done differently, it's hard to predict how the pregnancy rate for the female condom will compare with that of other barrier methods in the long run. After more data are collected, it is possible that the FDA will allow changes in the labeling with regard to pregnancy rate.

Barrier methods in general have higher pregnancy rates than methods such as the Pill or IUDs. Based on limited data, the female condom seems to have a slightly higher pregnancy rate than male condoms, and about the same pregnancy rate as diaphragms, cervical caps, and sponges (which are no longer available in this country as of this writing). Women who use no method at all have about an 85 percent chance of getting pregnant in a year.

Like the male condom, the female condom should provide significant protection against sexually transmitted diseases. In laboratory testing, the polyurethane female condom did not let any STD-causing germs through, including viruses, the tiniest of these invaders. However, there are, so far, limited scientific data available about STD protection when the female condom is used in normal circumstances by regular human beings. Because it covers more body area than a diaphragm or cervical cap, and doesn't allow any contact between a woman and the man's semen, this method may prove to provide more protection against at least some types of STDs (including HIV, the virus that causes AIDS) than those barrier methods.

How Much It Costs

Reality condoms cost a lot more than male condoms—about seven or eight dollars for a box of three. They may cost less if you get them from a family planning clinic or college health service.

The Advantages of This Method

Unlike male condoms, this method is used by women, giving them a new means of control over their sexual health.

The female condom can be inserted into the vagina before sex, so some people find that it interrupts sex less than male condoms (which can only be put on after a man has an erection).

Men (and women) may find they like the softer, looser feel of the female condom more than the tight male condom.

People who are allergic to latex (the material most condoms, diaphragms, and cervical caps are made of) can use this method.

The female condom should provide significant protection against many types of sexually transmitted diseases, including HIV, the virus that causes AIDS.

The Disadvantages of This Method

The female condom is new and odd-looking, which may make some people reluctant to give it a try. (Think back, though, to the first time you saw a male condom; they are not exactly elegant, either.)

Like all barrier methods, female condoms only work— protecting you against pregnancy and sexually transmitted diseases—when you use them. You have to have one ready and waiting—in your purse, in your bedside-table drawer— when you are ready to have sex.

Because of the possibility of human error, barrier methods in general have higher pregnancy rates than methods such as IUDs, the Pill, or Norplant.

You are likely to be more aware of the female condom during sex (especially the first couple of times you use it) than you would be with other methods, including other barrier methods. For example you and your partner will probably be aware of the outer ring shifting as you move. Both men and women have complained of pubic irritation.

Reversibility

This method is immediately reversible. If you don't use it, even once, you could get pregnant.

Tips for Using Female Condoms

■ This is a relatively new method that people may not be familiar with. Be sure to read the instructions that come in every box (and have your partner read them, too, so that he knows what to expect) before trying to use the female condom for the first time.

■ Getting the condom in and out can be a little tricky at first. It might be a good idea to practice a few times by yourself so that you don't give up in frustration or embarrassment the first time you try to use it with your partner. (Throw the "practice" condom away because it will have come in contact with your vaginal secretions.)

■ It's a good idea to hold the man's penis and guide it into the condom. That way you can be sure the penis is inside the condom (not next to it), and that the condom's outer ring doesn't get pushed into the vagina.

■ You can use extra lubricant with the condom if the man feels as if it's sticking to or "riding" his penis during sex. (Female condoms come with a small bottle of extra lubricant.) The lubricant can be put either on the condom or on the penis.

■ If the condom "squeaks" or feels like it's rubbing either partner, try adding a few drops of lubricant or moving into a slightly different position.

■ Use extra lubricant on the outer ring if it feels as if it might be pushed inside the vagina during sex. If the outer ring does go into the vagina, the package insert recommends that you stop, remove the condom, and put in a new one before continuing.

■ Don't try to use a male condom and a female condom at the same time: According to the instructions they may stick together.

- Be careful not to snag and tear the condom on teeth, fingernails, or jewelry.

- If you keep extra condoms on hand and don't have sex for a while, be sure to check the expiration date on the box before you start to use them again.

- All of the above will probably get a lot easier once you and your partner have tried this new method a few times.

- If you have any problems with or questions about the female condom, ask your doctor or someone at your family planning clinic or health service, or call the free phone number on the Reality female condom box: 1-800-274-6601.

Safety and Side Effects

This method is very safe. It has no effect on anything inside a woman's body—it doesn't affect your menstrual cycle or your natural hormones. It doesn't require the use of any additional chemicals (such as spermicide), as the cervical cap and diaphragm do. There is nothing about this method that would be expected to have any effect on a fetus if you did accidentally conceive while using it. Polyurethane has not been reported to cause allergic reactions.

Who Is a Good Candidate for This Method

Women (or couples) who want to protect themselves against pregnancy and sexually transmitted diseases.

Women who are willing to use the female condom every time they have sex.

Women who can afford this relatively expensive barrier method.

Couples who find they enjoy using this method more than male condoms.

Women who have sex infrequently and don't want, or need, the everyday protection of methods such as the Pill or an IUD.

Who Is Not a Good Candidate for This Method

Women who would find it hard to use female condoms correctly and consistently. A big part of consistent use is having your contraceptive where you are when you need it. Also key: a willing partner.

Those who find the condom's appearance unappealing.

Men or women who experience rubbing or irritation from the outer ring.

CHAPTER

7

VAGINAL SPERMICIDES

Currently Available

Vaginal spermicides are widely available without a prescription at drugstores, supermarkets, and so on. They come in a variety of forms, including

- Foams (popular brands include Emko, Delfin, Koromex)
- Creams and jellies (such as Ortho Gynol II, Koromex, Conceptrol)
- "Inserts," or suppositories (such as Semicid and Encare)
- "Film" (vaginal contraceptive film, or VCF, is not as widely available as the other forms of spermicide)
- Spermicide-saturated sponges (the Today vaginal contraceptive sponge was discontinued in 1995 due to manufacturing problems and as of this writing is no longer available in the United States)

Most of the spermicides available in this country contain the sperm-immobilizing ingredient nonoxynol-9. A few contain a very similar chemical called octoxynol. Some spermicides are designed to be used alone, other packages indicate that the product is meant to be used with a diaphragm or cervical cap, but there is not really much difference between them.

Approximately 3 percent of women rely on spermicides for birth control, according to the Ortho 1995 Annual Birth Control Study.

What It Is

Unlike other barrier methods, spermicides (used alone) provide a chemical barrier, rather than a physical one, against conception. (Vaginal sponges did offer both, when they were available.) Spermicides are designed to be placed in the vagina to kill the sperm before they can reach and fertilize a woman's egg.

How It Works

Spermicides are chemical "surfactants." Much the way surfactants in your laundry detergent dissolve greasy stains, the surfactants in spermicide dissolve the fatty components in the membrane that covers the sperm, which kills them.

Whatever type of spermicide you choose (foam, cream, etc.), it must be inserted into the vagina, as close to the cervix as possible, before any contact with the man's penis. Foams, creams, and jellies start to work as soon as you put them in, and stay active for about an hour. Inserts and vaginal films take about ten to fifteen minutes after you put them in to melt and disperse before they become fully effective. (Encare may cause a feeling of warmth in the vagina as it foams and expands.) Since time and other specifics do vary, be sure to read the package and follow the instructions before you use any type of spermicide.

If you have sex more than once, or if you wait more than an hour before having sex, most package instructions say that you should put in another dose of spermicide. If you are using the spermicide with a diaphragm (see chapter 8), the instructions usually tell you to insert another dose into the vagina (without removing the diaphragm) if you have sex again before it's time to take the diaphragm out. If you are using your spermicide with a cervical cap (see chapter 9), the instructions usually say additional spermicide is not required, although it certainly can't hurt, and may help maintain effectiveness. If these recommendations sound a bit vague, they are. Spermicides simply haven't been subjected to the kind of intense, long-term scientific scrutiny that newer, more "high-tech" prescription methods such as the Pill, the ParaGard IUD, Norplant, and Depo-Provera have undergone. The recommendations that do exist are based on limited scientific data—combined of course with large doses of the experts' common sense and decades of practical experience.

How Effective It Is

Used alone, vaginal spermicides tend to have high failure rates. Of one hundred typical users, about twenty-one are likely to get pregnant during one year of use. If spermicides were used according to directions every time a couple had sex, the pregnancy rate would probably be substantially lower— more on the order of six pregnancies in those one hundred couples. That's still twice as many as for perfect use of condoms, but much fewer than if no method is used: If those one hundred couples used no method for a year, eighty-five of them would be expected to get pregnant.

These numbers, it should be noted, are estimates, unlike the more precisely known failure rates quoted for methods such as the Pill, Norplant, IUDs, and Depo-Provera—or even condoms—all of which, as explained above, have been studied more extensively and in more scientifically exacting ways than have spermicides alone.

Spermicides used together with condoms are more effective than either method used alone.

As for sexually transmitted diseases, spermicides have been shown to be able to kill the germs that cause most common STDs in a test tube. Although it's likely that they do provide some measure of protection in real-life use, it is impossible to say exactly how much. Unlike condoms, spermicides are not allowed by the FDA to claim protection against STDs on their packages and labels. There is also a complicating factor here: There have been studies showing that very frequent, prolonged use of spermicide (the original studies were done on prostitutes in Africa) seem to be associated with sores on the walls of the vagina—which could theoretically end up making women more vulnerable to infection, rather than less. While this probably does not happen with the amounts of spermicide most people use most of the time, until more studies are done, it is impossible to say for sure exactly how much spermicide it might take to have this effect.

How Much It Costs

As with condoms, how much this method costs will depend on how often you have sex. Although prices vary, depending on the type of spermicide you buy and where you buy it, you will probably end up spending about twenty-five cents per dose. That would add up to about twenty-five dollars a year, or less, if you had sex an average of twice a week and only used spermicides.

The Advantages of This Method

Spermicides are widely available at supermarkets, drugstores, and convenience stores.

They require no prescription and no doctor visit for a woman to be able to use them.

They are very safe. They do not affect menstruation or a woman's natural hormone cycle.

They are relatively inexpensive.

You can buy as much or as little as you need, and only when you need birth control.

Unlike with condoms, a woman can use this method without a man's cooperation, although he will probably be aware that you are using it.

The Disadvantages of This Method

As with all barrier methods, you have to use spermicides every time you have sex. However, you can apply spermicide to the vagina before intercourse, so it doesn't interrupt lovemaking the way condoms can.

Spermicides used alone tend to have high failure rates—higher than with other barrier methods that provide a physical barrier between egg and sperm, and significantly higher than with methods such as the Pill and IUD.

The chemicals in spermicides can cause irritation in one or both partners.

Spermicides alone provide much less protection against STDs than condoms.

Reversibility

Spermicides are immediately reversible. If you use them, you are protected against pregnancy. If you don't use them, even once, you could get pregnant.

Safety and Side Effects

Spermicides are very safe and are not known to have any systemic effects. There may be some absorption into the body (there have been reports of Encare causing a soapy taste in some women's mouths, for example), but this has never been shown to be harmful in any way.

Sometimes spermicides cause irritation. You or your partner might notice an itching or burning sensation on your genitals. Sometimes people think that they have a urinary tract infection or a vaginal infection and it takes them a while to figure out that the spermicide is causing their symptoms. If one brand or formulation bothers you or your partner, it's possible that a different one might not.

A number of years ago there was a widely publicized report suggesting a possible link between spermicide use early in pregnancy and birth defects. This report has been criticized for its design and analysis—it was a retrospective study that relied on women's memories of having bought spermicide in the six months before they got pregnant. Today the consensus of expert opinion is that there does not appear to be a cause-and-effect link between spermicides and birth defects. If you are worried about this possibility, discuss it with your doctor.

As discussed above, there is the possibility that prolonged use of large amounts of spermicide might cause sores in the vagina and increase the risk of transmission of some types of

TIPS FOR EFFECTIVE SPERMICIDE USE

■ As with all barrier methods, spermicides work only when you use them.

■ Always insert the spermicide as close to the cervix as possible.

■ Wash your hands before inserting a spermicide. If there is an inserter, also wash that with soap and water after you use it.

■ Be sure to give the spermicide time to foam or melt, if necessary, before you have sex. How long you have to wait after insertion varies from type to type: Be sure to read the package insert of the kind you buy.

■ Apply more spermicide if you wait more than an hour to have sex.

■ Apply more spermicide if you have sex more than once.

■ Keep an extra package handy so that you don't run out unexpectedly.

■ If one form or brand of spermicide is irritating to either you or your partner, try a different one. If it still bothers you, you will probably have to consider other contraceptive options.

■ Don't douche after sex for at least six hours, or you may lower the spermicide's effectiveness. Douching does not work as a contraceptive. Most doctors consider it unnecessary at best. If you feel better after douching, talk to your doctor about the safest way to do so.

sexually transmitted diseases. This is probably not a problem when spermicides are used as most people do—one, possibly two doses, several times a week.

Who Is a Good Candidate for This Method

Women who have the discipline to use spermicides consistently and correctly every time they have sex. Spermicides can be kept on hand even if you regularly use another method. They can be used along with methods such as fertility awareness or condoms for an extra measure of protection against an unplanned pregnancy. You can also use spermicide as a backup if you miss more than one birth control pill.

Who Is Not a Good Candidate for This Method

Women who would find it difficult to use spermicides every time they have sex. It takes discipline to use this and other barrier methods.

Because of the typically high failure rate, women who have medical reasons that could make a pregnancy dangerous should seriously consider more effective methods.

DIAPHRAGMS

Currently Available

Koro-Flex Arcing Spring Diaphragm (London International U.S. Holdings)

Koromex Coil Spring Diaphragm (London International U.S. Holdings)

All-Flex Arcing Spring Diaphragm (Ortho-McNeil Pharmaceutical)

Ortho Coil Spring Diaphragm (Ortho-McNeil Pharmaceutical)

As of 1995 about 1.7 million (3 percent) women in this country used a diaphragm, according to the Ortho 1995 Annual Birth Control Study. This method is most likely to be used by married women between the ages of thirty and thirty-nine. Two-thirds of the women who use this method have done so for at least five years.

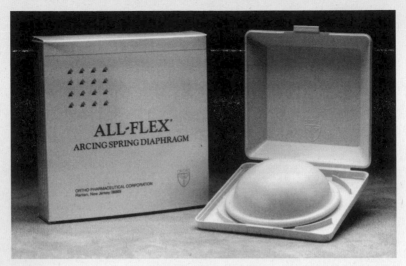

(Used by permission of Ortho-McNeil Pharmaceutical)

THE DIAPHRAGM

What It Is

A soft natural rubber (latex) device, shaped like a shallow bowl, with a firm but bendable rim. The rim is designed to fold so that the diaphragm can be slipped into the vagina. As soon as you let go, the diaphragm opens to cover the cervix.

Diaphragms are designed to be used with spermicide. Before insertion, about a teaspoon of spermicide is placed into the bowl of the diaphragm and a small additional amount is spread around the rim.

Diaphragms are available by prescription only, since they must be sized to each woman individually by a doctor or health professional in order to fit—and therefore work—properly.

How It Works

The diaphragm works in two ways. First, it serves as a physical barrier that covers the cervix to keep sperm from entering the uterus and tubes, where they might fertilize an egg. Second, the bowl of the diaphragm holds the spermicide and keeps it concentrated around the cervix.

Unlike a condom, which must be put on a man's erect penis during sex, a woman can put in her diaphragm before—even hours before—having sex. To insert it, hold the diaphragm rim up, squeeze the rim flat with one hand, hold the vaginal lips open with your other hand and slip the diaphragm into the vagina. (Wash your hands first.) Push the front of the rim with one finger until it slips into place behind the pubic bone. When it's in the right place, the spermicide-filled dome of the diaphragm will be covering the cervix. You should be able to feel the cervix through the rubber.

After you have sex, you must leave the diaphragm in place for six hours to give the spermicide time to kill all the sperm. To remove the diaphragm, hook a finger under the rim and gently pull it out. If you have sex again before the six hours is up, just insert more spermicide into your vagina, leaving the diaphragm in place. Start counting the hours to removal from the last time you have sex.

After removing the diaphragm wash it with mild soap and water. Be sure to rinse it well, since soap could damage the rubber if left on the diaphragm for a long time. Dry it thoroughly and put it back in its case to protect it from damage. Over time your diaphragm may become stained or discolored. As long as there are no holes in it (you should check for holes every time you use it), the diaphragm will still work.

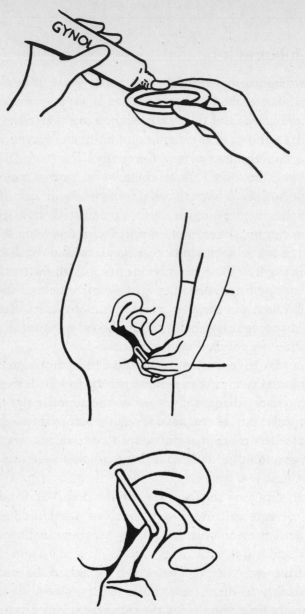

(Used by permission of Ortho-McNeil Pharmaceutical)

INSERTING THE DIAPHRAGM

How Effective It Is

Diaphragms, like natural methods of family planning and other barrier methods, are frequently subject to human error. If one hundred women used their diaphragms perfectly (according to directions every time you have sex) for one year, about six of those women would get pregnant. That's a higher pregnancy rate than would be expected with perfect use of condoms. More typically about eighteen out of one hundred women become pregnant in a year of using the diaphragm.

Younger women at peak fertility are more likely to have a failure with this method (and other barrier and natural methods) than are older women whose fertility is declining. After about age forty, women gradually start to ovulate less frequently, and as time goes by, the eggs they release are less likely to be healthy enough to be fertilized, or to make a healthy embryo if they are fertilized.

Women who have sex frequently (twice a week or more) are also at higher risk of pregnancy with this method, because they are likely to have sex close to the time of ovulation. If any sperm evade the spermicide, they can live in the tubes and uterus for several days, waiting for an egg to come along.

It can be helpful for women who use this and other barrier methods to be familiar with the techniques of natural fertility control, such as observing the natural changes in your cervical mucus. That way you can use your body's signs of peak fertility as a reminder to be extra diligent about using your diaphragm exactly right.

Perhaps surprisingly, there is little solid scientific evidence to show exactly how long spermicide remains active. To really be on the safe side, then—and even though package instructions often say you can put in the diaphragm up to six hours ahead of time—you may want to consider putting additional spermicide into the vagina (without taking the diaphragm out) if you wait more than an hour or so to have sex.

In order to work effectively, the diaphragm must be fitted properly by a doctor or trained health professional. The goal is to get the largest size possible that is not uncomfortable to insert and can't be felt once it's in place. If the diaphragm is too small, it may move around too much in the vagina and let sperm sneak by; if it's too big, it may press against the urethra (the tube through which urine exits the body) and possibly contribute to urinary tract infections. Although it can be hard to do so, it's important to try to relax as much as possible while the diaphragm is being fitted, otherwise you might end up with a too-small size.

The type of spring on the diaphragm (arcing spring, coil spring) is largely a matter of personal preference, but sometimes depends on internal physical characteristics (such as the size and position of organs and internal muscle tone). Some experts feel that an arcing rim (which compresses anywhere you pinch it) is the easiest for women to put in correctly. However, this type of diaphragm cannot be used with an inserter—a plastic holder—which some women prefer.

To ensure the best possible fit—and therefore maintain the highest possible effectiveness while you use this method—your doctor should check your diaphragm's size if you gain or lose more than about ten pounds, if you have vaginal or pelvic surgery, or if you have a baby or an abortion. Even if none of the above apply, it's a good idea to double-check the fit when you see your doctor for your routine exams.

How Much It Costs

A diaphragm costs about twenty dollars and, as long as it doesn't develop any holes, can be used for about two or three years. Spermicide costs about twenty-five cents per use. In considering the total cost of this method, remember that you have to see a doctor to have it sized correctly in the first place and that you should have the fit checked yearly. (Simple size rechecks shouldn't add much, if anything, to the cost of a regular gynecologic checkup.)

The Advantages of This Method

Safety and immediate reversibility rank high on this method's list of advantages.

This method (unlike condoms) is entirely within a woman's control: You can put it in well before sex and be protected against pregnancy.

As with all barrier methods, you only need to use this method when you have sex. (Unlike the Pill, which you have to take every day, even if your partner's on a business trip for two weeks; or Norplant, which stays put until you take it out, whether or not you even have a partner.)

Studies have shown that using a diaphragm plus spermicide can cut approximately in half a woman's risk of sexually transmitted diseases and pelvic inflammatory disease, a serious infection that can result from undetected infections. Diaphragm users have also been reported to have a lower risk of cervical abnormalities and cervical cancer. In a test tube, spermicides have been shown to kill the germs that cause many sexually transmitted diseases, including gonorrhea, herpes, and HIV. However, studies (on prostitutes) have shown that very frequent use of unusually large quantities of spermicides may result in sores in the vagina, which theoretically might increase the risk of HIV infection. Further studies under more normal circumstances are needed to clarify the relationship between HIV susceptibility and spermicide use. (See also chapter 7, "Vaginal Spermicides, Safety and Side Effects.")

The Disadvantages of This Method

Probably the biggest disadvantage of this method (and one that is true of all barrier methods) is that you have to be very motivated to use the diaphragm correctly and consistently every time you have sex.

The diaphragm is available by prescription only. You must go to a private doctor or family planning clinic or college health service to have the device individually fitted: Diaphragms come in a variety of sizes and with one of two types of springs in the rim (which makes a difference in how they fold for insertion).

Some women find it hard to insert the diaphragm—the process can be uncomfortable, or the device can fail to slip into proper position. Coil-spring diaphragms can be used with an inserter, which some women find makes them easier to put in. Sometimes getting it in isn't the problem, but getting it out is. Squatting (or sitting on the toilet) and straining (pushing) as if for a bowel movement can help move the diaphragm lower in the pelvis and make it easier to remove.

Some who try it complain that the diaphragm is messy and interferes with the spontaneity of sex. Certainly this method isn't for everyone. But couples who have used diaphragms successfully usually find ways around the potential problems and find that the drawbacks are outweighed by the advantages. As we've noted, a diaphragm doesn't interfere with sex if you put it in well beforehand. (If you don't end up using it, you can just take it out again.) Some couples find it perfectly acceptable to incorporate diaphragm insertion into foreplay itself, as one does with condoms. If you find that the spermicide makes everything too slippery, maybe you're using too much—or maybe another brand, or a cream formulation instead of a jelly would work better for you.

Reversibility

The diaphragm is an immediately reversible method of birth control. If you use it, you are protected against pregnancy; if you don't, you aren't. It's totally up to you.

Safety and Side Effects

The diaphragm is generally considered to be a very safe method of birth control.

About ten years ago there was an unsettling study that suggested spermicides might cause birth defects if accidentally used early in pregnancy. Since then other studies have not supported this report, and most experts are now convinced that spermicides do not cause birth defects. The original report has come under a great deal of criticism for the way it was designed and for the conclusions it reached.

A small percentage of the population will have an allergic reaction to latex, or natural rubber, which will mean they can't use this contraceptive. (These are the same people who also won't be able to use latex condoms or cervical caps.)

Some people are sensitive to spermicides, which would cause itching or burning when they're used. This sensitivity can occur in either partner. There is also, as mentioned above, the currently unresolved question of whether using very large amounts of spermicide over long periods of time might cause sores or ulcers on the walls of the vagina and the cervix.

There have been reports suggesting that diaphragms might increase the risk of urinary tract infections, especially if they are not fitted properly. Call your doctor if you have the following symptoms, which can indicate an infection: pain when you urinate, blood in the urine, fever, feeling like you have to urinate all the time even if nothing comes out. Most urinary

TIPS FOR SUCCESSFUL DIAPHRAGM USE

■ Putting the diaphragm in and taking it out can take a bit of getting used to. Be sure you are comfortable doing this and that you know how to check that it's in the proper position *before you leave the doctor's office or clinic.* Once at home, try inserting and removing the diaphragm in different positions (standing with one foot on a chair, squatting, lying on your back) to see which you find easiest and most comfortable.

■ Wash your hands before putting the diaphragm in or taking it out. Don't get petroleum jelly (Vaseline) or any skin creams containing oils on the diaphragm, since this can weaken the rubber.

■ For the diaphragm to work, it must be in the right place: covering your cervix. After you put it in, you should be able to feel your cervix (a firm protrusion at the top of the vagina) through the rubber dome of the diaphragm.

■ Try changing positions during sex if you or your partner can feel the rim of the diaphragm.

■ If you're worried that this method will make sex less spontaneous, remember that you can put the diaphragm in ahead of time.

■ If the diaphragm is too slippery to grasp and squeeze flat, you may be putting too much spermicide around the rim.

■ It's a good idea to keep extra spermicide (and even an extra diaphragm) on hand in case you need it on short notice.

■ Use more spermicide if you have sex again before it's time to take the diaphragm out. Don't move the diaphragm. Leave it where it is and simply put the spermicide into the vagina.

> ■ Package instructions usually say to insert more spermicide into the vagina if you wait longer than six hours to have sex. To be on the safe side (since nobody really knows exactly how long spermicides remain active), you might want to put in the extra dose if only an hour or so has gone by.
>
> ■ Check the diaphragm when you wash it to make sure there aren't any rips, holes, or worn-out-looking areas. If the diaphragm starts to look worn, replace it.

tract infections are easily treated and respond quickly to prescription antibiotics.

There is also some concern about the possibility that the diaphragm might increase a woman's risk of toxic shock syndrome (TSS), which most people have heard about in connection with tampon use. There have been a few cases reported in the literature in which this apparently has happened, and the possibility is mentioned in the package insert. Although toxic shock is rare, it can be deadly. For this reason anyone who has had toxic shock in the past should not use this method. It is possible that leaving the diaphragm in the vagina for long periods of time might increase the risk of TSS. You are supposed to leave the diaphragm in for six hours after the last time you have sex—but after that, to be on the safe side, you should try to take it out as soon as possible. The package instructions say you shouldn't leave it in for more than twenty-four hours. The symptoms of toxic shock can include a sudden high fever, vomiting, diarrhea, faintness, and a sunburnlike rash. Joints and muscles may ache and the eyes may redden. If you suddenly spike a fever and have even one of the other symptoms, take out the diaphragm immediately and call your doctor.

Who Is a Good Candidate for This Method

Highly motivated women who are willing to use this method every time they have sex.

Older women in stable relationships. Because fertility is past its peak, the risk of unintended pregnancy is lower for these women. Long-standing couples may also have the time and motivation to work out some of the kinks of diaphragm use, such as when and where to put it in and take it out.

Women whose lives are predictable enough, or who are good enough at planning ahead, to know that the diaphragm will be where they are when they need it.

Women who have medical reasons for not using the Pill or an IUD.

Women who are familiar with this method can also use it (instead of condoms) as a backup if they forget to take a birth control pill.

Who Is Not a Good Candidate for This Method

Couples who would find it hard to use their diaphragm every time they wanted to have sex.

Women who are highly fertile and have sex frequently, since this and other barrier and natural methods may have too high a failure rate.

Women who are not comfortable touching their genitals.

Women who have recurring urinary tract infections when they use the diaphragm.

Any woman who has had toxic shock syndrome in the past.

CERVICAL CAPS

Currently Available

The Prentif Cavity-Rim cervical cap was approved by the FDA for use in the United States in 1988. It is manufactured by Lamberts, Ltd., in Luton, England, and distributed in the United States by Cervical Cap Ltd., in Los Gatos, California.

Far fewer women (and doctors) in this country know about cervical caps than its barrier-contraceptive cousin, the diaphragm. The device is more popular in England and is also available in European countries, including France and Switzerland, as well as in Canada and Australia.

What It Is

A thimble-shaped device made of natural latex rubber (the same material as most diaphragms and condoms) that is designed to fit closely over a woman's cervix. The cup part of the cap is soft and flexible, the rim is firm, and about one and one-half inches wide. There is a groove on the inside rim of the cap that creates a seal against the cervix and helps hold it in place.

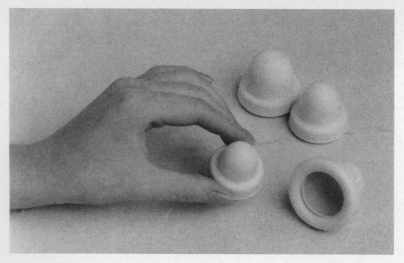

(Cervical Cap Ltd.)

THE CERVICAL CAP

Like diaphragms, cervical caps come in different sizes, and you need to go to a doctor or family planning clinic to have one fitted for you.

Cervical caps are used with spermicide. You fill the cup about one-third full before inserting it.

How It Works

The cervical cap works in two ways. It is a physical barrier that fits closely over the cervix, preventing sperm from entering. It also works as a holder for spermicide, keeping this additional chemical barrier concentrated close to the cervix, where it's most needed. Because it must be precisely the right size to hug the cervix, not all women can be properly fitted with a cervical cap. The fit must be more exact than with a diaphragm.

To insert the cap, squeeze the rim flat with one hand while holding your vaginal lips apart with your other hand. (Wash your hands first.) Gently push the cap, rim end first, into the vagina and as far up as it can go, until it covers the cervix. If the cap doesn't slip into place, you can either try to push it over the cervix with your fingers or you can take it out and start over again. When the cap is in right, it completely covers the cervix—run a finger around the rim to check. It also won't come off easily if you push it with a finger, or when the penis bumps it during sex. You should also be able to feel the cervix through the rubber dome of the cap. The dome won't be tight against the cervix, since there has to be a little space to hold the spermicide and any secretions from the cervix.

You must leave the cap in place for eight hours after the last time you have sex to be sure that any sperm that manage to get into the cap have been killed by the spermicide. The longest you should leave the cap in is forty-eight hours, according to the package instructions, because of a possible risk of toxic shock syndrome.

The cervical cap instructions say you don't have to put in more spermicide if you have sex more than once. However, there's a lack of good scientific data showing precisely how long spermicide actually stays active in the cap, so it certainly can't hurt—and may well give you an extra edge of protection—if you do use more. Insert extra spermicide into the vagina without moving (or removing) the cap.

To get the cap off the cervix when it's time to remove it, use a finger to gently break the seal between cap and cervix, then pull the cap down and out of the vagina. Squatting and bearing down (as if pushing out a bowel movement) can help make the cap easier to reach. Wash the cap in mild soap and warm water, and rinse and dry it well, before you put it away.

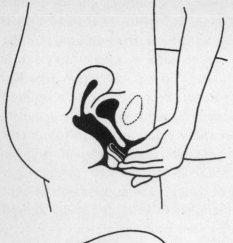

Hold cap pinching the sides together. Reach back to place cap on the cervix.

Check placement of the cap with index and middle finger. The cervix should be completely covered by the cap. The dome should feel soft with some dimpling.

(Cervical Cap Ltd.)

INSERTING THE CERVICAL CAP

How Effective It Is

It is hard to be precise about how well the cap prevents pregnancy, in part because it has not been used, or studied, all that much in this country and in part because effectiveness seems to vary greatly from woman to woman, depending on variables such as how well the cap fits and how diligently she uses it.

According to *Contraceptive Technology*, among women who have not had children, about eighteen out of every one hundred would typically get pregnant during a year of using the cervical cap. Used correctly every time, the cap's failure rate in this group drops to about nine in one hundred. The cap may be significantly less effective in women who have had children: Typical failure rates are listed at 36 percent; perfect use at 26 percent. The Prentif Cap's package insert says it's between 82.6 and 93.6 percent effective, "depending on consistency of use."

There really isn't a lot of good scientific evidence that directly compares barrier methods to one another. Scientifically it's not considered accurate to compare the results of separate studies, since researchers don't all use the same rules and standards; instead the contraceptives should be compared directly in the same study so that the same conditions would apply to each method.

Used consistently and correctly, male latex condoms plus vaginal spermicide are generally considered to be more effective in preventing pregnancy than the cervical cap plus spermicide. Nonbarrier contraceptives such as Norplant and IUDs have higher "typical" effectiveness ratings, because once they're in place, they work. Remember, many, if not most, failures with barrier methods occur primarily because people *don't* use them correctly and consistently.

The cervical cap and spermicide will provide some protection against sexually transmitted diseases, although it's hard to know exactly how much. It would be logical to expect the cap to provide less protection (at least against certain diseases) than the male or female condom, since condoms prevent direct contact between penis and vagina, while the cap only covers the cervix.

How Much It Costs

Cervical caps cost about the same as diaphragms—around twenty dollars for the device alone. Because you have to go to a clinic or private doctor to have the cap properly fitted and to learn how to put it in and take it out, you will need to take into account this cost too. As long as the cap is in good shape, it can be used for up to three years before you replace it.

Cervical caps are used with spermicide. This additional cost (about twenty-five cents per use) will depend on how frequently you have sex. Twice a week would add up to about twenty-five dollars a year.

The Advantages of This Method

The cervical cap can be used by a woman and does not require a man's cooperation.

This method can be put in hours ahead of time if you want to, so it doesn't interrupt sex.

The cervical cap can be left in place for up to forty-eight hours, although it sometimes causes an odor problem with prolonged use. During that time you can have sex as many times as you want. (With all other barrier methods you have to either apply more spermicide or use another condom each time you have sex. However, even for this method, adding spermicide each time you have sex could give you an extra edge of effectiveness.)

This method has no known bodywide effects. It does not change a woman's hormone levels, and it does not affect menstruation or fertility.

The Disadvantages of This Method

Although it does provide some protection, the cervical cap does not defend against sexually transmitted diseases as well as latex male condoms do.

As with the diaphragm, you have to go to a doctor to have the cap fitted correctly.

It can be difficult to find a doctor who is knowledgeable about fitting caps and how to use them.

Some women find the cervical cap difficult to put in and take out (more so than the diaphragm).

This method cannot be used during menstruation. It also cannot be used by a woman who has a vaginal or cervical infection or bleeding, or an abnormal Pap smear result, or until six weeks after a woman has a baby, a miscarriage, or an abortion.

Some men report that they can feel the cervical cap during sex.

This method has a higher failure rate than many other kinds of contraceptives.

Reversibility

The cervical cap is immediately and completely reversible. Any time you don't use it, you could get pregnant.

Safety and Side Effects

The cervical cap is generally a very safe contraceptive that causes no systemic side effects.

Some women have abnormal Pap smear results (microscopic changes in cervical cells) when they use the cap. You will have to switch to another method of birth control if this condition persists. When you get a cap, your doctor will probably ask you to come in for a Pap smear after about three months, just to be sure everything's okay.

A small number of women and their partners are sensitive to latex and will be unable to use this method. Some people are also sensitive or allergic to spermicides.

There has been some suggestion that using a cervical cap might increase a woman's risk of toxic shock syndrome, a rare but potentially fatal illness. (This is the same type of toxic shock that has been reported with tampon use.) It is not known how much a cap user's risk is increased, or if in fact it is actually increased at all. To be on the safe side, the cap is approved for use for no longer than forty-eight hours, on the theory that prolonged use increases risk. Any woman using a cervical cap (or diaphragm or tampons) should be familiar with the symptoms of toxic shock: sudden high fever; fainting or dizziness; sore throat; muscle aches and pains; red, sunburnlike rash. Remove the cap and call your doctor immediately if these symptoms occur.

Who Is a Good Candidate for This Method

Women who will be able to use this method consistently and correctly every time they have sex.

Women who can get the hang of putting the cap in and taking it out.

This method might work well for women who have sex mostly on the weekends, since you can leave it in place for up to forty-eight hours.

A cervical cap might be a good choice for older, slightly less fertile women in stable relationships who don't want to use methods such as the Pill or an IUD and who would feel comfortable working through the "learning period" necessary with this method.

Who Is Not a Good Candidate for This Method

Women who can't get a proper fit with the cap.

Women who have trouble putting the cap in and taking it out. Many find this harder to do than with a diaphragm. If you can't use it easily, a cap is unlikely to be a good choice for you.

Women who are sensitive to spermicides (they cause burning or itching) or to latex, or whose partners are sensitive to spermicides or latex.

Women who develop cervical problems (i.e., abnormal Pap smear results) when they use the cap.

Any woman who has had toxic shock syndrome.

Any woman who has undiagnosed vaginal bleeding or a vaginal or cervical infection, until it is treated and clears up.

Any woman who has had a baby, a miscarriage, or an abortion in the past six weeks, because the shape and/or size of the cervix may change.

Women who have medical reasons that would make a pregnancy dangerous. Such women should carefully consider whether any barrier method is the best possible choice for them, because of their relatively high failure rates . If it is the best option, study up on the fertility awareness methods discussed in chapter 4; using them in conjunction with a barrier method may help you decrease the risk of accidental pregnancy.

TIPS FOR SUCCESSFUL CERVICAL CAP USE

■ Be sure you are comfortable with inserting and removing the cap and that you know how to check that it's in proper position *before you leave your clinic or doctor's office.*

■ Once you get home, try putting the cap in and taking it out in different positions (squatting, standing with one leg on a chair, lying on your back) to see which is easiest for you.

■ The package instructions suggest using a backup method (such as condoms) for about a week at home while you and your partner get used to the new method. Check the cap before and after sex to make sure it stays in position. If it comes off, you may need a different size: Don't use the cap any more until you see your doctor again. (If you find out after sex that the cap has been dislodged, you may want to check with your doctor about whether emergency contraception—see chapter 17— might be indicated in your particular situation.)

■ Always wash your hands before inserting the cap; and don't let anything oil-based (including petroleum jelly, baby oil, many skin creams, and some vaginal medications) touch it. Oil makes latex deteriorate quickly.

■ Before you put it in, check the cap for holes or tears.

■ Always use spermicide along with your cervical cap. Although the method doesn't require it, you may want to apply more spermicide for extra protection before repeating sex.

■ Don't forget to take the cervical cap out. It is likely to cause a bad odor, and may possibly increase your risk of toxic shock syndrome, if you don't.

■   A Pap smear after three months of cervical cap use is recommended. If the results are abnormal, you will need to switch to another method, at least temporarily.

■   Have condoms available to use during menstruation.

■   Remember, for this method (or any barrier contraceptive) to work, you have to use it every time you have sex.

Part Four

HORMONE-BASED METHODS

10

ORAL CONTRACEPTIVES— "THE PILL"

Currently Available

There are dozens of oral contraceptives currently available in this country. Forty-seven different brand names are listed in the 1995 *Physicians' Desk Reference* (PDR), a tome that lists and describes almost all of the drugs that are currently approved by the Food and Drug Administration (FDA) in the United States. Despite what might seem like a daunting number of options, most pills are actually quite similar, and some brands vary only in their packaging or nonactive ingredients.

The Pill is used by over 50 million women around the world, and more than 16 million in this country alone. More women in the United States use oral contraceptives than any other method of birth control. According to the Ortho 1995 Annual Birth Control Study, about one in every four women (26 percent) who currently uses birth control is on the Pill.

Oral contraceptives are available by prescription only. You

must see a doctor and have a health history taken and a physical exam before the Pill can be prescribed.

What It Is

Oral contraceptives contain a combination of two hormones—an estrogen and a progestin. Both are synthetic, or man-made, versions of the two female sex hormones, estrogen and progesterone, which are produced by the ovaries every month during the menstrual cycle.

Today the vast majority of the pills available in the United States contain the man-made estrogen ethinyl estradiol. A few contain the estrogen mestranol, which is converted in the body into ethinyl estradiol.

Pills may contain one of several different synthetic progestins. Commonly used "classic" or older-type progestins include norethindrone, norethindrone acetate, and levonorgestrel. There are also several "new" progestins, such as desogestrel and norgestimate, now available in some pills. This recent generation of progestins was designed to be very potent at low doses and have a minimum of undesirable effects, although there are very new data indicating a possible increased risk of blood clots with desogestrel (see "Safety and Side Effects").

(There is also a type of pill, known as the "minipill," which contains *only* a progestin, no estrogen. Because the effectiveness, safety, and side effects of the minipill are different in many ways, it is discussed separately in chapter 11.)

Most women today take oral contraceptives that contain 35 micrograms or less of estrogen. These are commonly referred to as "low-dose" pills, because they contain significantly less hormone than earlier versions of the Pill. Several popular pills in the 1960s, for example, contained a whopping 100 micrograms of estrogen. That's almost three times more estrogen than today's most popular formulations. This is important because the health risks of oral contraceptives (and in fact most drugs) are generally dose-related: In other words, the lower the dose, the less likely the side effects.

Most birth control pills contain the same amount of estrogen and progestin in each tablet. There is also a type of pill in which the amount of hormone varies during the month— another strategy aimed at minimizing the total hormone dose while maintaining a high level of effectiveness. Popular varieties of this type of pill include Ortho-Novum 7/7/7, which has three different progestin levels, and Triphasil (Wyeth-Ayerst) in which both the estrogen and progestin levels vary. Your doctor will help you decide which oral contraceptive formulation would be best for you.

Don't be too concerned about selecting exactly the right pill out of the seeming sea of choices. Most of the birth control pills available today are more similar than they are different, and any number of pills containing 30 to 35 micrograms of estrogen (making it qualify as a "low-dose" pill) will probably work just fine for most women. Only in certain situations will a specific formulation possibly make a difference. For instance, if you are on a regular low-dose pill and your blood level of LDL (low-density lipoprotein—the "bad" cholesterol) goes up, as sometimes happens, a triphasic pill may have less effect on your cholesterol levels. Women who are bothered by persistent minor side effects that are usually blamed on estrogen, such as breast tenderness or nausea, may find relief with a very low dose pill (in the 20 microgram range). The trade-off is that breakthrough bleeding is more common with very low dose pills. Both triphasic and very low dose pills may have less margin for error in terms of pregnancy risk if you occasionally forget pills. Women who suffer from what are commonly referred to as androgenic side effects, such as increased body hair or acne, may find relief if they switch to a pill with a different progestin, or to a triphasic, which averages out to a lower progestin level overall.

No matter what type of pill your doctor prescribes, each pack will contain twenty-one active pills—that is, twenty-one tablets that contain hormones. If you use a twenty-one-day pack, you take the pills for three weeks and then take one week off before starting the next pack. Most manufacturers also offer twenty-eight-day packs, for women who find it easier to remember to take their pills if they can do so every day without a break. If you use a twenty-eight-day pack, the first twenty-one pills are the active (hormone-containing) tablets, and the last seven, which are a different color, are inactive placebos ("sugar pills" or "reminder pills").

How It Works

The hormones in oral contraceptives stop ovulation by acting on the pituitary gland to suppress FSH and LH (follicle-stimulating hormone and luteinizing hormone). Some people say the Pill works by "mimicking pregnancy," because with the steady hormone input from the pills, your brain never receives the signal to start maturing new eggs each month. If there are no eggs, you can't get pregnant. In addition the progestin in the Pill makes the cervical mucus thicker, so it's harder for sperm to get through, and it makes the lining of the uterus thin and unable to support the growth of a fertilized egg, in the unlikely event that there is one.

To make pill taking as easy as possible to keep track of, it is often suggested that you start taking your first pack of pills on the Sunday after your menstrual bleeding starts. If your period starts on a Sunday, you take your first pill that day.

You should then take another pill every day, at about the same time of day, until the pack is used up. Some women like this schedule because they usually won't have menstrual bleeding on the weekends.

Another approach favored by some doctors and manufacturers is to start taking your first pack of pills on the first day of menstrual bleeding ("day 1" of the menstrual cycle), no matter what day of the week that is. That way the pills will start to suppress ovulation before the egg-maturing process has a chance to begin that month. Some experts do recommend that women who prefer the Sunday-start use a backup method of contraception for at least a week or two of the first cycle, in case ovulation occurs before the pills take full effect. Talk to your doctor about which strategy might be best for you.

If you use a twenty-one-day pill-pack, you will take one pill daily for three weeks (twenty-one days), then take one week off before starting the next pill-pack. Most women will start to bleed about two or three days after taking their last pill. Without the steady hormone input from the pills, the endometrium will slough off, just as it does after hormone levels drop naturally at the end of a menstrual cycle. Women on oral contraceptives usually find that their periods are lighter, shorter, and are accompanied by less pain and cramping. Lighter bleeding is due to the fact that the Pill supplies both estrogen and progesterone (which has a growth-inhibiting effect on the uterine lining) throughout the month, so the uterine lining never gets as thick as it might naturally.

If you use a twenty-eight-day pack, start a new pack the next day after your last one runs out: On this regimen you take a pill every day, without a week off. Expect your period during the week that you take the different-color "reminder" pills.

In order to keep the level of hormone in your system as steady as possible (which maximizes effectiveness), it is important to take your pills as close to the same time every day as possible—ideally within about an hour.

If you forget to take pills, particularly early in a pill-pack, the amount of hormone in your body drops too low and you may ovulate. Be sure to get instructions from your doctor about what to do if you forget pills. Many experts advise women simply to take a single forgotten pill as soon as you remember it. It's okay to take two at the same time if you don't realize you've forgotten one until you go to take the next day's pill. After that go back to taking pills one at a time until the pack is finished. If you only miss one pill, your risk of pregnancy is still quite small. (If you forget to take one of the inactive "reminder" pills in a twenty-eight-day pack, just throw it away. Since these pills do not have any hormones in them, you don't need them to maintain the Pill's protection against pregnancy.)

If you forget two or more pills, your doctor will probably want you to call and talk about what to do. Most likely you will have to use a backup contraceptive method (such as condoms) for the rest of that cycle. Depending on how many pills you've missed, and where you are in your cycle, you may be told not to take the rest of that pill-pack, and you may need a pregnancy test before starting to take your pills again. If you find yourself missing pills often, you should consider changing to a different method—possibly a long-acting method such as Norplant or Depo-Provera or a ParaGard IUD (see chapters 12, 13, and 14). Birth control pills work well only if you take them regularly.

How Effective It Is

Most pregnancies occur when women forget to take their pills. Birth control pills work by keeping a steady amount of hormones in your body that suppress ovulation. In clinical studies—where pill users were carefully selected, counseled, and supported—fewer than one in one hundred women who took their pills every day without fail got pregnant in a year of using this method. Since most women don't have that kind of intensive support, typically about three women out of one hundred will get pregnant in a year.

How Much It Costs

The pill isn't cheap. Expect to pay about eighteen to twenty dollars a month for each pill-pack. If cost is a significant factor, you may be able to get pills for less through a family planning clinic, such as Planned Parenthood. However, you can't just walk in with a prescription and pick up a pack of pills. The clinic will want to take a medical history and do a physical exam first, just as if you went to a new private doctor for the first time.

The Advantages of This Method

Oral contraceptives are highly effective. Women who take their pills correctly and consistently get pregnant at a rate of less than one in one hundred per year.

Women who are on the Pill have very regular and predictable periods. They bleed less, for fewer days, and have less pain and cramping. Women who like the Pill consider this a big plus of Pill use. In practical terms you don't have to worry as much about leaking blood, or about cramps interfering with work or fun, and you have fewer "days off" from sex if you or your partner don't like to have intercourse during your period.

The Pill also has some very important noncontraceptive health benefits. Women who used to have heavy periods will be at less risk for anemia (a decrease in the blood's oxygen-carrying red cells) while they're taking the Pill. Pill users are less prone to benign breast disease (noncancerous fibrous lumps and fluid-filled cysts), ovarian cysts, and pelvic inflammatory disease (a sometimes dangerous infection that can lead to infertility). The risk of potentially life-threatening ectopic, or tubal, pregnancy is much lower.

The Pill also cuts approximately in half a woman's risk of two important female cancers—those of the endometrium (the lining of the uterus) and the ovary. Endometrial cancer is the most common gynecologic cancer in this country; and ovarian cancer, because it is so hard to detect early, is the gynecologic cancer that more women die from each year than any other. The protective effect may last as long as ten years after you stop taking the Pill.

The Disadvantages of This Method

For this method to be effective, you have to be able to remember to take your pills every day. Most failures—unplanned pregnancies—occur when women miss pills. Some women find it easier to remember to take a pill every day without a pause between packs of pills: For them, twenty-eight-day pill-packs may be a good choice.

The expense of this method will be a significant disadvantage for some women.

You have to take the Pill every day, no matter how frequently—or infrequently—you have sex.

Birth control pills do not protect a woman against sexually

transmitted diseases, including herpes, chlamydia, and HIV, the incurable virus that causes AIDS. However, studies have shown that women who take the Pill do have a lower-than-average risk of pelvic inflammatory disease (PID). This infection of the upper reproductive tract (uterus, fallopian tubes, etc.) can be serious and may lead to infertility. Experts speculate that progestin's effect of thickening the cervical mucus may help keep disease-causing germs confined to the vagina. Women who are at risk for STDs should use a condom, or have their partners use a condom.

Birth control pills aren't for everyone. Some women can't safely use them because of certain health conditions (see "Safety and Side Effects," on the following page).

Reversibility

In most women fertility quickly returns to normal. Some women experience a slight delay. Women who had irregular periods before going on the Pill are likely to find that their cycles become irregular again after they discontinue taking it. Because irregular cycles can be an indication of lowered fertility, these women may have trouble getting pregnant after they stop taking oral contraceptives. In other words the Pill doesn't cause fertility problems in these women, but it can temporarily mask fertility problems that previously existed.

There is a lingering myth that women need to wait a certain period of time after going off the Pill before trying to conceive. This is not necessary. Women who get pregnant immediately should not worry that leftover hormones in their systems could harm their babies: The hormones in the Pill are metabolized and excreted from the body within a few days.

Women who do not wish to become pregnant when they

stop taking the Pill need to start using another method of birth control immediately.

"Pill breaks," which used to be suggested sometimes to allow the body to reestablish "natural" menstrual cycles, are not necessary or recommended. It's all too easy to get pregnant during the switch to or from another method. The original source of the "break" misconception probably evolved from the fact that the Pill was originally approved for use for only two years. (By the time that two years was up, by the way, approval had already been extended.) Now all time restrictions have been removed from the labeling. As long as you remain healthy (i.e., you don't develop health problems that would make Pill use riskier, such as uncontrolled high blood pressure, elevated cholesterol, heart disease), and as long as you don't smoke, most experts now agree that you can safely continue using oral contraceptives until you reach menopause and no longer need birth control. Your health and your risk factors are the primary concern, not your age.

Safety and Side Effects

It is often said that more scientific data have been collected about oral contraceptives than any other drug in history. Yet women probably have more misconceptions about the safety of the Pill than they do about almost any other type of medication.

For example, surveys have shown that most women think the Pill is pretty risky—they believe it's quite likely to cause conditions such as heart attack, stroke, or cancer. The fact is that while serious side effects do occur, they are not common, particularly among healthy young women, and particularly when those women use the low-dose pills available today. When the Pill was first approved in the 1960s, it contained much higher doses of hormones. It was also given to women who would not be considered good candidates for the Pill to-day—such as smokers over age thirty-five. As the amount of hormone in the pills has gone down over the years, and as doctors have become more selective about prescribing the Pill, the frequency of serious problems related to Pill use has also gone down.

Most women with fibroid tumors of the uterus can safely take birth control pills. Studies have shown that low-dose pills generally have no effect (either positive or negative) on these noncancerous growths.

Most studies have shown no increase in birth defects in women who conceive accidentally while on the Pill, even if they continued taking the pills for weeks before they realized they were pregnant. While early package inserts for the Pill did mention the possibility of "fetal anomalies," this warning was later removed.

In general, to keep all risks as low as possible, women should be on the lowest dose Pill that is acceptable to them—meaning one that does not cause problems such as "break-through bleeding," or spotting between periods, and that maintains a high level of contraceptive effectiveness. As the estrogen dose goes down, side effects go down as well, but at the same time pregnancy rates start to edge up. For most women a pill with 30 or 35 micrograms of estrogen will be a good choice.

MINOR SIDE EFFECTS. The Pill has a number of fairly common side effects that are not a problem health-wise but can be bothersome. In fact most women who decide to stop using the Pill do so because of one of these symptoms, not for medical reasons.

Nausea can occur, particularly during the first three months of Pill use. Taking your pill with a small snack or just before a meal can help. Light spotting or staining sometimes occurs between periods. Again this is most common during the first few months of Pill use, and usually diminishes month by month. If spotting persists, or if it is heavy—or simply if it worries you—talk to your doctor. (Be sure to keep taking your pills unless your doctor instructs you to stop; and if you stop, be sure you have another method of birth control available if you don't want to get pregnant.) If spotting doesn't get better after a few months, you may want to consider switching to a different Pill formula.

You may also experience missed periods. Women who have been taking their pills regularly should be reassured that this is not harmful to your body. But if you have missed pills, or if you have any symptoms of pregnancy (nausea, breast tenderness), let your doctor know, since you could be pregnant. If you're worried about a possible pregnancy, you can do a home pregnancy test. If you are pregnant, you should stop taking the pills.

Other minor side effects include breast tenderness, more frequent headaches, and water retention (sometimes fingers and ankles can swell). Many women worry about gaining weight on the Pill. However, studies have shown that as many women lose pounds as put them on. Because water retention can even affect the corneas of the eyes, some contact lens wearers may have trouble when they go on the Pill. A darkening of the skin called melasma can occur, but this is much less common with today's low-dose pills and can be avoided if you use sunblock.

A negative effect on cholesterol (specifically an increase in the "bad" LDL cholesterol) can occur in some Pill users. Today's low-dose formulations are less likely to have this effect than were older, high-dose pills. Triphasics may have less of an effect than regular low-dose pills.

DRUG INTERACTIONS. There is good evidence that the antituberculosis drug rifampin can increase breakthrough bleeding and the risk of pregnancy in Pill users. It has been suggested that certain antibiotics and antiseizure medications may also reduce the Pill's efficacy, although these interactions have not been as clearly documented in clinical studies. Be sure to tell any doctor you see that you are on the Pill, and ask about possible interactions if you are given a prescription.

Since the Pill can change the results of some lab tests, you should also tell any doctor who orders lab tests that you are taking the Pill.

SERIOUS HEALTH RISKS. Women on the Pill are more likely to form blood clots in their veins, most often in the legs, than are women who are not taking oral contraceptives. In some cases part of the clot may break off, travel in the bloodstream to vital organs, then get stuck and block critical blood flow. If a clot lodges in the brain, it can cause a stroke; if it gets stuck in a lung, it is called a pulmonary embolism; if it blocks blood flow to an eye, it can cause blindness. This does not happen often, but it does happen. The risk of blood clots goes up for *all* women just after a pregnancy, during prolonged bed rest, and after major surgery. In these situations it may be safer to switch to another method of contraception, at least temporarily.

As this book went to press, several very new studies suggested that at least two of the "new" generation of progestins (desogestrel and gestodene, which is not available in the United States) may put women at approximately double the risk of nonfatal blood clots in their veins, compared to women on pills containing "traditional" progestins like norethindrone, norethindrone acetate, ethinyldiol diacetate, and levonorgestrel. (Another new progestin, norgestimate, was not implicated.)

Although it will probably be some time before this issue is resolved, women taking pills containing desogestrel should know that the risk of clots is still very low—on the order of 1 or 2 per 10,000 women per year, which is lower than the risk during pregnancy or with earlier high-dose pills.

The risk of other cardiovascular problems (heart attack, stroke) may be increased in Pill users, but most experts have concluded that this risk is very low.

Smoking significantly increases the risk of cardiovascular problems. You must tell your doctor that you smoke if you are considering this method of birth control. Be honest with your doctor about how much you smoke: That is the only way he or she can advise you accurately about the risks. Any woman who is on the Pill should do her utmost to stop smoking. (Of course for health reasons that go far beyond Pill risks, *every* smoker should strive to quit.) Since the risk of heart disease increases with age, the Pill is not recommended for women over thirty-five who smoke.

The Pill may also increase your risk of the following: a rare form of liver cancer and noncancerous liver tumors, and possibly gallbladder disease (studies are conflicting on this one).

Many women worry that the Pill causes cancer. As explained on page 122 (in the "Advantages" section), it actually provides significant protection against endometrial and ovarian cancers. However, breast cancer is one area of concern. According to the research available at this time, it appears that Pill use does not increase women's risk of breast cancer overall. But as a recent report from the National Cancer Institute (NCI) explains, there is growing evidence that there may be an increased risk of developing breast cancer at a young age (before thirty-five or forty), particularly among women who take the Pill for a number of years, starting in their teens or early twenties.

At this point many questions remain. For example, might

the Pill actually trigger cancers? Or instead could it somehow promote the growth of cancers that already exist? And if young women take the Pill and *don't* get cancer by age thirty-five or so (and there are millions of such women walking around today), might they turn out to be less likely than average to get breast cancer later? At this point nobody knows the answers. Intensive research is ongoing in this area, and perhaps a clearer picture of the risk will begin to emerge over the next few years. If you are concerned about this issue, talk it over with your doctor. Keep in mind that even if this link is eventually proven, breast cancer is so uncommon in women this young that the actual number affected would be quite small: The NCI has estimated that the additional risk might be on the order of 1 per 100,000 women a year.

Every pill-pack comes with a detailed package insert. It is important to read this information carefully (some of it may sound quite frightening) and talk over anything that worries you with your doctor.

Who Is a Good Candidate for This Method

Women who want a highly effective, readily available, easily reversible method of contraception.

Women who can remember to take their pills every day.

Most women over the age of forty who don't smoke and who have no risk factors.

Teenagers who are sexually active, once they have established regular menstrual cycles and have had their growth spurt. Women with multiple partners also need to protect themselves against STDs with condoms. The possible increase in the risk of breast cancer in young women appears to be small and should not deter you from taking the Pill if this is otherwise a good contraceptive choice.

TIPS FOR WOMEN TAKING THE PILL

■ To make it easier to remember to take your pills, link pill taking to something you already do at the same time every day, such as brushing your teeth before you go to bed.

■ Taking the pills with a small snack can help head off the mild nausea some women get during the first few months of Pill use.

■ Keep an extra pill-pack on hand so that you won't run out.

■ Keep a backup contraceptive (such as condoms and foam) on hand, too, in case you forget pills, need to stop taking them for some reason, or their effectiveness is reduced (if for example, you have been vomiting with the flu, or need to take a course of antibiotics for an infection).

■ Keep the name of your prescription in your wallet in case you need to be able to tell a doctor what type of Pill you're taking.

■ Let any doctor you see know that you are on the Pill.

Women with fibroid tumors of the uterus can usually use the Pill with no problems.

Women with endometriosis. They may even find that Pill use improves their condition.

Women with heavy periods. They may find that oral contraceptives decrease bleeding and cramping.

Young women with a strong family history of ovarian cancer may be encouraged to use oral contraceptives, since this method significantly reduces the risk of this malignancy.

DANGER SIGNS

Serious problems in women who take the Pill are not common. But when they do happen, they can require emergency care. Report the following to your doctor immediately:

- Pain or swelling in one leg
- Severe abdominal pain
- Sharp or severe chest or arm pain
- Sudden shortness of breath
- Severe headaches, or persistent headaches that don't respond to over-the-counter pain relievers
- Slurred speech
- Tingling or weakness on one side of the body
- Blurred or double or loss of vision
- Depression (lack of energy, mood changes)
- Yellowing of the skin or eyes, dark urine, light stools (all signs of jaundice)

Women with irregular periods due to polycystic ovarian disease. The Pill may help normalize their menstrual cycles, reduce the risk of endometrial cancer, and relieve some of the androgenic effects (acne, hair loss, body hair growth) of this condition.

Who Is Not a Good Candidate for This Method

Women with very hectic lives or unpredictable schedules, who would find it hard to be able to take a pill at the same time every day.

Women who have just had a baby. They should wait at

least a month before starting the Pill. If you're breastfeeding, wait until you've weaned the baby before taking the Pill.

Women who, despite reassurance and careful assessment of their individual risks, are still afraid that the Pill isn't safe. Birth control is supposed to make your life easier, more under control; this method won't be worth it if you're going to worry that every little twitch and twinge means that some obscure and horrifying side effect is about to strike.

The Pill is contraindicated (meaning physicians should not prescribe it) for women who have or have had blood clots in their legs or elsewhere.

Women who have had a stroke or a heart attack, certain benign liver tumors, or liver cancer also should not use the Pill. According to the package insert, it should also not be used by women who have or have had breast cancer or any cancer that might grow if exposed to estrogen.

Women with undiagnosed vaginal bleeding cannot use the Pill until the condition is diagnosed and treated.

Women who have had jaundice of pregnancy or jaundice with Pill use should choose a different contraception.

Women who are pregnant.

The Pill is not recommended for women over thirty-five who smoke, because smoking greatly increases the risk of heart attack and stroke.

Women with the following conditions should be followed with special care by their doctors if they choose the Pill: diabetes, high blood pressure, elevated cholesterol or triglycerides, migraines, epilepsy, or depression.

CHAPTER

11

PROGESTIN-ONLY "MINIPILLS"

Currently Available

Micronor (Ortho)
Ovrette (Wyeth-Ayerst)
Nor QD (Searle)

Since most surveys and studies don't separate out mini-pill users from those who take the more familiar "combined" estrogen-progestin oral contraceptives (see chapter 10), it is hard to be precise about how many women use the minipill. Probably only about 1 percent of Pill users in the United States choose progestin-only oral contraceptives, according to one recent report from Family Health International in the medical journal *Contraception*. The minipill is somewhat more popular in the Scandinavian countries and Great Britain, particularly among older women.

Minipills, like all hormone-containing contraceptives, are available by prescription only. You must have a health history taken and a physical exam done by a doctor before you can get minipills.

What It Is

A type of birth control pill that contains only one hormone: a man-made progestin, which is very similar to the natural hormone progesterone that is made by a woman's ovaries. The same two progestins found in minipills (norgestrel and norethindrone) are also used along with estrogen in some "combination" oral contraceptives. There is no estrogen in minipills.

How It Works

Minipills contain a very small dose of progestin, about one-third the amount contained in some of the most popular combined (estrogen and progestin) oral contraceptives. They can go this low because minipills are designed to be taken every day, without a break. (Combined oral contraceptives, in contrast, are taken daily for three weeks, followed by a hormone-free week—during which you take either no pills or the different-colored inactive pills in a twenty-eight-day pack.)

Minipills have several different effects on the body that work together to reduce the possibility of pregnancy. First, they suppress ovulation, the release of a mature egg from the ovary, approximately half the time. Progestin also makes the cervical mucus very thick and sticky, so sperm are unlikely to get to an egg and fertilize it, if in fact an egg is released. Finally, the minipill slows the movement of the egg through the tubes and makes the lining of the uterus thin and unreceptive. (The other progestin-only contraceptives, Depo-Provera and Norplant, which are discussed in chapters 12 and 13, work essentially the same way, although the extent to which they suppress ovulation differs somewhat.)

When you start to use minipills, you take the first pill on

the first day of menstrual bleeding. If you're switching from combined oral contraceptives, take your first minipill the day after the last active pill in your pill-pack (don't take any of the inactive "reminder" pills if you've been using a twenty-eight-day Pill). If you have a miscarriage or an abortion, you can start the pills the next day.

Once you start, you take another pill every single day for as long as you continue to use this method. Because there is no break from the hormone, most women don't have regular periods on minipills. Instead light, irregular bleeding at any time of the month, or no bleeding at all, are common.

Since the amount of hormone in these pills is so small, each dose reaches its peak level in the bloodstream very quickly. A few hours later it's already dropping. Therefore it is very important that you take your pills as close as possible to the same time each day so that the hormone level doesn't drop too low to be effective.

If you take a pill as little as three hours late, or vomit soon after taking a pill, some experts recommend using a backup method (such as condoms) for two or three days. If you miss one pill, you will probably be instructed to take it as soon as you remember; and then take the next pill at the usual time, and use a backup method for two or three days if you have sex. If you miss more than one pill, ask your doctor whether you should stop taking your pills or not (expert recommendations vary). Even if you do continue taking your pills, you will probably be told to use a backup method for about two weeks. Your doctor may also suggest a pregnancy test if you miss pills. If you find that you often forget pills or take them late, you should consider switching to another birth control method that doesn't require such precision timing.

If you have irregular bleeding, don't stop taking the pills. If you don't bleed at all for two months, you might want to do a home pregnancy test and/or talk to your doctor, since there's a possibility you might be pregnant, particularly if you forgot or were late with pills.

How Effective It Is

Pregnancy rates are higher with the minipill than for combined pills or Norplant or Depo-Provera. According to the proposed new labeling information for minipills, the perfect-use failure rate in the first year is 0.5 percent, or one in two hundred users. Typical pregnancy rates would be expected to be closer to 5 percent, or five per one hundred users.

How Much It Costs

Minipills cost about the same as combination (estrogen-progestin) pills. A single pill-pack will cost about eighteen to twenty dollars a month. If price is a big concern, you might want to go to a family planning clinic, such as Planned Parenthood. Of course the clinic will want to take your health history and do a physical exam before prescribing this, or any other, method of birth control. Just like a private doctor, clinics need to be sure that the contraceptive you want (even if you've been using it already) is really the best, healthiest choice for you.

The Advantages of This Method

The low dose of hormone (low progestin, no estrogen) in minipills is considered a significant advantage in terms of safety.

Unlike the other progestin-only methods (Norplant and Depo-Provera), you can stop taking minipills at any time, without a visit to the doctor. Remember, though, that if you do go off the pills, and you don't want to get pregnant, you must start using another birth control method immediately.

Minipills (and the other progestin-only methods) can be used by women who are breastfeeding. Combined oral contraceptives may decrease milk production and are generally not recommended for nursing mothers. A small amount of progestin does get into the mother's milk with minipills, but this has not been shown to cause any harm to the child. Women who are nursing tend to be naturally less fertile, so the fact that minipills are somewhat less effective than other hormonal methods may be less of a problem at this time.

Women who use progestin-only methods usually lose less blood during the month (so this method might be a good choice if you tend to bleed heavily and are prone to anemia), although bleeding is more likely to be irregular and somewhat unpredictable. Minipill users also report less menstrual pain and less of the midcycle pain that can be associated with ovulation. (With combined oral contraceptives periods are also lighter and less painful; but they are very predictable.)

This method may be appropriate for some women who, for health reasons, can't take estrogen.

The Disadvantages of This Method

Minipills frequently cause irregular bleeding. Because unpredictable bleeding—which is often no more than light spotting or staining—can be disconcerting, this is one of the most common reasons women stop using this method. The same is true of the other progestin-only methods, too. If you choose one of these contraceptives, you should know that irregular bleeding is not harmful to your body; nor is it a sign that your method isn't working properly, assuming you have been taking your pills regularly.

Minipills have a significantly higher failure rate than the other progestin-only contraceptives. That's because you can't "forget" your Norplant or Depo once you've gotten them, but it is all too easy to forget to take a pill every single day at the same time. Because the dose of progestin is so low in the minipill, it can make a big difference in your chances of getting pregnant if you forget to take even one tablet. This is, in short, a method that doesn't have much margin of error.

This method provides no protection against sexually transmitted diseases, including common infections such as herpes and chlamydia and the less prevalent but deadly HIV, the virus that causes AIDS. However, there is evidence that minipills may reduce the risk of pelvic inflammatory disease (PID), possibly because the thickened cervical mucus forms a physical barrier that helps keep germs from traveling up into the uterus and tubes. If you have sex with more than one man (or if your partner has sex with others), use a condom to reduce the risk of infection.

Some women have medical conditions that make them unable to use this method.

Reversibility

Women who stop taking minipills quickly become fertile again. Remember, this is a method for which some experts suggest using a backup if you are just hours late taking your pill. The slightly delayed return to fertility that sometimes happens with combined pills is less likely with minipills.

There is no "waiting period" after going off minipills. Women who would like to get pregnant can start trying to conceive immediately.

Women who do not want to get pregnant need to start using another type of contraceptive the same day they stop taking minipills.

Safety and Side Effects

Because minipills are much less commonly used than combination pills, there are less scientific data on their safety and side effects. Combined oral contraceptives are, by comparison, one of the most thoroughly studied drugs available.

Theoretically minipills should be safer than combined pills because they contain no estrogen, and only a small dose of progestin. Progestin-only contraceptives were actually developed as a way of trying to avoid some of the cardiovascular problems that have been associated with estrogen use—such as blood clots in the veins, stroke, and heart attack. However, because there were fairly limited data on side effects when these pills were approved, for many years the package insert listed most, if not all, of the same contraindications as for combination oral contraceptives. (One of the most difficult things about studying the side effects of birth control is that serious problems are unusual. Which means that when they do occur, it can be nearly impossible to determine whether the problem was actually related to hormone use, or whether it would have happened anyway.) Since minipills were first approved, more information has been gathered about them, and many experts now feel that blood clots in the veins, heart attack, and stroke should not be contraindications to minipill use. Minipill experts, the FDA, and drug companies have been discussing changes in the labeling for some time. Very recently at least one minipill company has revised its package insert, eliminating many of the risks associated with estrogen.

As with other progestin-only methods, women who use

minipills have a slightly increased risk of ovarian cysts. These fluid-filled sacs on the ovary are totally benign (noncancerous), but they can become large enough to cause lower abdominal pain. Normally a cyst will go away without treatment in about four to six weeks. In rare cases a cyst will rupture or become twisted and require surgery.

According to the package information, some studies have shown an increase in headaches, breast tenderness, nausea, and dizziness in minipill users. So-called "androgenic effects"—excess body-hair growth, acne, weight gain—are possible but not common with minipills.

Women who are on minipills should be alert to abdominal pain, however, since there is a small chance that the cause could be an ectopic (tubal) pregnancy instead of a simple cyst. As is true of other progestin contraceptives, as well as with the IUD, if you do get pregnant, you have an increased risk that the pregnancy will be ectopic. And while ectopic pregnancies are not common among those who use these methods of birth control, they can be dangerous. It is important to report to your doctor any persistent abdominal pain that doesn't respond to regular over-the-counter medication, especially if it continues to get worse, suddenly becomes severe, or is accompanied by dizziness or fainting.

There is no known increase in the risk of birth defects in babies born to women who conceived accidentally while taking minipills. Of course women should stop taking the pills immediately once they do realize they are pregnant.

There are drugs that can make minipills less effective, including antiseizure medications such as phenytoin (Dilantin), carbamazepine (Tegretol) and phenobarbital, and the tuberculosis drug rifampin. According to the new package information, no significant interaction is known to occur with antibiotics. Be sure to let any doctor who prescribes medication for you know that you are on progestin-only birth control pills. Similarly, if a doctor orders lab tests or blood work for you, let him or her know that you are taking progestin-only oral contraceptives.

Be sure to read the package-insert information that comes with every package of oral contraceptives. Ask your doctor about anything you don't understand, or anything that worries you. Only your own doctor can put the risks into perspective for you as an individual.

Who Is a Good Candidate for This Method

Some women who want to use oral contraceptives but cannot take estrogen may be able to safely take minipills.

Minipills might be a good choice if you want a quickly reversible method to use between planned pregnancies.

Women who are breastfeeding a baby can use minipills. Minipills have been used by nursing mothers around the world for decades, and there is no evidence of any negative effects on the baby. Milk production is not decreased in women taking minipills, as it can be in women using combination pills. Minipills might be a good "in-between" method, for use while you are still nursing but also supplementing with a bottle (in which case you may start ovulating again and need contraceptive protection). Then after your baby is completely weaned, you might switch to (or go back on) combined oral contraceptives for their higher effectiveness.

Some older women may find minipills to be a good option. The fact that minipills are slightly less effective than combined pills may be less of a problem at this point, since fertility naturally declines with age. Also, since minipills contain such a low dose of progestin, and no estrogen, they are considered by at least some experts in the field to be safer than combined oral

contraceptives, particularly in terms of the risk of thrombophlebitis (inflammation and clot formation in the leg veins).
One potential problem: Irregular bleeding, which is common
in minipill users, can sometimes be a symptom of other problems (the most worrisome being endometrial cancer) in older
women. Usually problem bleeding will be heavier and crampier
than the light spotting expected with minipills.

Some women who get severe breast tenderness, nausea,
and/or headaches when they take estrogen can successfully
take minipills.

Some women who develop hypertension on combination
oral contraceptives may not have the same problem with
progestin-only pills.

Who Is Not a Good Candidate for This Method

Women who would have trouble remembering to take a
pill at the same time every day. This could be a particular concern if you frequently travel across time zones, have a job
with shift changes, or if your daily schedule is hectic and
unpredictable.

Women who take antiseizure medication or other drugs that
can reduce the effectiveness of progestin-only contraceptives.

Women who have abnormal vaginal bleeding, until the
problem is diagnosed and treated.

Women who have had breast cancer should not take minipills, according to the package insert.

Women who would worry about pregnancy or other health
problems if their periods were irregular or absent will probably not be happy with this method.

CHAPTER

12

NORPLANT—
UNDER-THE-SKIN
CONTRACEPTION

Currently Available

Norplant is currently the only method of its kind: a contraceptive implant system. It is made in Finland by a company called Leiras Oy, and marketed in the United States by Wyeth-Ayerst Laboratories. Norplant was approved for use in the United States by the Food and Drug Administration (FDA) in 1990. As this book went to press, at least one new implant was nearing FDA approval, so it is possible that others will be available by the time you read this. The new implants—a two-rod system from the makers of Norplant and Implanon (Organon, Inc.)—are discussed in more detail in chapter 18, "Future Contraceptives."

As of 1995 approximately 1 percent of the birth control users in this country chose Norplant. That's about the same as the IUD (see chapter 14) and Depo-Provera injections (chapter 13). In contrast, about one in four birth control users is currently on the Pill (chapter 10), according to the Ortho 1995 Annual Birth Control Study.

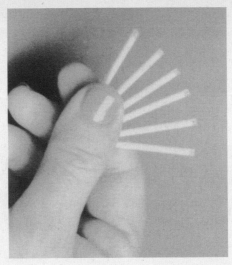

(Photograph courtesy of Wyeth-Ayerst Laboratories)

THE NORPLANT SYSTEM

What It Is

Six matchstick-sized Silastic capsules containing levonorgestrel, a man-made progestin. The same hormone is used in many popular birth control pills, and it is very similar to the progesterone that is made naturally by a woman's ovaries.

Norplant is available only by prescription. It must be put in and taken out by a trained doctor or health professional.

How It Works

The soft, flexible capsules are slipped just under the skin of the inner, upper arm in a fan shape. All of the capsules can be put in, one at a time, through the same tiny incision. Once it's in place, the active ingredient is slowly and steadily released for five years.

The progestin in Norplant has several different effects on the female body that together make pregnancy very unlikely. One thing it does is make ovulation (the release of a mature egg from the ovary) much less frequent. It doesn't stop it altogether, but fewer eggs released mean fewer chances for you to get pregnant. (Norplant suppresses ovulation about 75 percent of the time for the first couple of years, then about 40 to 50 percent of the time after that.) Progestin also makes the cervical mucus thick and sticky, so it's harder for sperm to get through; and it keeps the uterine lining thin and unreceptive to the implantation of a fertilized egg, in the unlikely event that there is one.

The insertion procedure is considered minor surgery and takes about fifteen minutes. Your doctor will use a bit of local anesthesia to minimize discomfort. Learning how to put the capsules in correctly and efficiently takes some practice, so you should have it done by a doctor who is familiar with Norplant, or by a health professional who is trained in the proper techniques for insertion and removal.

After the insertion the small incision will be covered with a bandage. No stitches are necessary. You should keep the area clean and dry for a day or two to minimize the risk of infection. You may have a bit of bruising and discomfort for a few days. After that the implant should not be uncomfortable at all. If it is, call your doctor: You might have an infection, which could cause one or more of the tubes to be expelled by your body. While you do need to be aware of this possibility, it's not something to worry about. Infection only happens in about one in two hundred insertions; prompt diagnosis and treatment minimize the risk of serious complications.

Norplant should be put in no more than seven days after you start a menstrual period, otherwise there is a risk of pregnancy. Timed this way, you won't need to use any other contraceptive after Norplant is in place. If you are currently using a barrier method and wish to start using Norplant, you should simply schedule your insertion for the appropriate time and use your condoms or diaphragm or cervical cap until the implants are in place. If you are using an IUD, you would have the Norplant put in during the week your period starts and have the IUD removed at the same time. If you are taking oral contraceptives, Norplant can be inserted at any time, but your doctor may want you to continue taking the Pill for a week, just to be safe.

How Effective It Is

Norplant is one of the most effective contraceptives available. It is nearly as effective as female sterilization, and about on a par with Depo-Provera and the ParaGard IUD. Over five years about 1 woman in 100 who uses Norplant will get pregnant; in the first year of use, only about 1 in 250 will. For this method the "perfect use" pregnancy rate is the same as the "typical use"—since, once it's in place, you can't misuse it or forget to use it.

Norplant does not protect you against sexually transmitted diseases (see "Disadvantages," below).

How Much It Costs

Norplant is pricey, at least to begin with. With this method almost all of the cost is up front—not spread out, as it would be if, for example, you bought a few packs of pills at a time over the same five years. The Norplant implants alone cost about $360. It will probably cost you upward of $500 to $700 once you add in the doctor's charge for an office visit and the insertion. However, if you were to continue to use Norplant for the full five years that it is effective, the yearly cost actually averages out to be a bit less than for birth control pills or Depo-Provera.

The cost is covered in every state by Medicaid. It is also covered, at least in part, by some private insurers and by some HMOs. In addition an organization called the Norplant Foundation provides the device free to some low-income women who do not qualify for Medicaid but could not otherwise afford it. (See the appendix for more information.)

The Advantages of This Method

Norplant is one of the most effective contraceptives available.

This method is also among the easiest for a woman to use. Once you have it inserted, you don't have to think about birth control again for as long as five years. Compare this to other hormonal methods: You have to take the Pill every day, without fail. You have to get injections of Depo-Provera every three months. Only the ParaGard IUD can protect a woman longer—up to ten years.

Most women using Norplant report fewer cramps and less pain with menstruation and midcycle (since they ovulate less frequently).

Norplant can be inserted immediately after an abortion or miscarriage. The package instructions say that nursing mothers can have Norplant put in when their babies are six weeks old. Some family planning clinics and doctors will insert the device earlier—as soon as milk flow is well established. Only a small amount of hormone, if any, gets into the mother's milk, and no harmful effects have been seen in the babies of mothers using Norplant. If you're not nursing, you can have Norplant inserted any time after delivery.

The Disadvantages of This Method

The initial cost, as explained above, must be considered a significant disadvantage.

Another factor that puts some women off is the fact that you have to go to a doctor's office or clinic to have the device inserted and removed. Some women don't like the idea of having any type of surgical procedure—no matter how minor—and others don't like the idea of having the capsules stay in their arms for years. (You can feel them, but you often can't see them under the skin.)

Norplant may not be as readily available to women as, for instance, birth control pills, both because of the cost and because of the training necessary to learn how to put it in and take it out. According to one recent survey, about 80 percent of Planned Parenthood clinics offer it. Hospital-based family planning clinics are also likely to have Norplant available. There is currently no way of tracking and reporting how many private physicians offer Norplant.

All of the birth control methods that rely on progestins alone (including the "minipill" and the injectable Depo-Provera) are likely to cause irregular bleeding. Irregular bleeding is the most common reason women decide to have Norplant removed in the first two years. The total amount of blood lost in a month is usually less than during a normal menstrual cycle; but it may be spread out over more days during the month, and come and go unpredictably. Amenorrhea (no bleeding at all) is also relatively common, especially during the first year of use. Some women are much more bothered than others by these changes in their menstrual cycles, especially if they weren't prepared for them ahead of time by their doctors. If you choose this method, it is important to understand that the bleeding changes are not harmful to your body, and they are not a sign that this method isn't working the way it should.

The package information says that Norplant may be less effective in women who weigh more than 154 pounds. In reality weight is probably not a major issue, for the following reason: Two different versions of Norplant (one with soft tubing, another with harder tubing) were used in the testing phases before Norplant was approved. Only the soft inserts have been used since approval. In studies using the harder tubes there was an increase in pregnancies in women who weighed more than 154 pounds after the first three years of use. This did not happen with the soft tubes during the initial studies, and has not happened in the full five years of studies on the soft tubes that have now been completed. However, to be on the safe side *all* of the original study data were included in preparing the original package insert, including the possibility of lowered effectiveness in heavy women. It is possible that the package insert will be updated at some point to include the more recent study results. Currently studies are looking at extending the use of Norplant for even longer than five years. It is possible that pregnancy rates may start to rise in heavier women with extended use before it does in smaller women, but so far this has not occurred.

Norplant will not protect you against sexually transmitted diseases, including gonorrhea, herpes, and deadly HIV, the virus that causes AIDS. However, the thickened cervical mucus provides a physical barrier that reduces to some extent the risk of pelvic inflammatory disease (PID), by making it harder for any germs to get through the cervix and travel up into the uterus and fallopian tubes. If you are using Norplant and are at risk for catching an STD, you or your partner should also use a condom.

Some women may be hesitant to choose this method

because of recent negative publicity. There are currently a number of lawsuits that have been filed for various reasons (most often problems with removal, some suggesting autoimmune or arthritislike reactions to the device) that have attracted quite a bit of media attention. If you've seen or read reports about Norplant that make you think you shouldn't use it (or that, if you are using it, you should have it removed), talk to your doctor. Many experts who have been involved in the research on Norplant feel that the negative publicity has greatly exaggerated the risks in the eyes of the public.

Reversibility

You can have the capsules taken out at any time. If you want to become pregnant or switch to another method of birth control, the capsules must be removed from the arm by a health care professional trained in the proper technique.

After Norplant is removed, any remaining drug is out of the body within about three days. Therefore it is important that you start using another contraceptive *immediately* if you don't want to get pregnant.

If you do want to conceive, it's safe to start trying right away. There is no recommended "waiting period" after the device is removed. Pregnancy rates are similar to those of women who have never used the device: About three-quarters will become pregnant within a year after Norplant is taken out.

Removing the capsules from the arm has proven to be more complicated than insertion. Expect it to take more time— probably about thirty minutes, depending, at least in part, on how much past experience your health care provider has in removing the device. It can take longer, and be more uncomfortable, if the capsules were inserted too deeply in the first place. Also some women's bodies naturally form more scar tissue around the capsules, which makes taking them out a bit harder. With adequate local anesthesia, removal should not be painful. Occasionally it will take more than one visit to the doctor's office to get all the capsules out. (A new version of Norplant—which has just two hormone-containing rods—is expected to be available in this country soon. Fewer capsules mean simpler insertion and removal.)

The incision will be slightly longer than the one that was done for insertion, but still less than half an inch (usually about one-half centimeter is enough). Once the rods are out, the area will be covered with a bandage and should be kept clean and dry for several days to avoid infection. There may be some temporary bruising and numbness, and you may be left with a small scar, which will fade over time.

The Norplant device is currently approved for five years of use. (Studies are showing that it may work longer, so at some point in the future it may be approved for six or more years.) If you have moved or changed doctors, you will need to remember when the five years are up and arrange for removal and—if you are not then trying to get pregnant—for continuing contraception. When the device is inserted, you should be given a card with the insertion and removal dates on it. Keep this card with your medical records. You can have another Norplant inserted, if you wish, for another five years of contraception. The five-year limit is on the device itself, because it eventually runs out of hormone; there is no time limit for how long a woman can use this method.

Safety and Side Effects

Norplant appears to be very safe. Although it has been on the market in this country for a relatively short time, it was studied extensively around the world before it was approved by the FDA. So far, during testing and early use, there have been remarkably few serious side effects reported.

The amount of progestin released by the capsules is very low, about the same amount as in the minipill. Most combined birth control pills contain four times as much progestin. Because Norplant contains no estrogen, researchers theorize that there should continue to be very few, if any, of the cardiovascular problems associated with estrogen use—such as venous thrombosis (blood clots in the veins). Although it is established that such problems increase as estrogen doses go up, it has never been clearly demonstrated that cardiovascular risks disappear entirely if only progestin is used. It is possible that they might occur with progestins, too, just less frequently; and very unusual side effects can take many years of widespread use to show up. So far there are simply not enough data on Norplant to give it an absolute all-clear. Right now the package insert for Norplant says that women who have *active* thrombophlebitis (inflammation of and clot formation in the leg veins) should not use the device.

There is an increased risk of ovarian cysts (fluid-filled pockets on the ovary) with Norplant and other progestin-only contraceptives. Normally these benign (noncancerous) swellings cause no problems and will go away by themselves in a month or two. Sometimes they can cause pain in the lower abdomen; very rarely surgery will be required to remove a cyst. Women should be alert to abdominal pain because there is also a very small chance that you could have an ectopic (tubal) pregnancy. Ectopic pregnancies can be life-threatening if not diagnosed and treated promptly. Fortunately they are also quite rare in women using Norplant because so few women get pregnant.

As mentioned above, irregular, unpredictable periods are

common. About three-quarters of women will have some type of change in the timing and/or the amount of bleeding. Heavy bleeding has been reported but is very uncommon. If you have been having regular periods (which indicate that you are likely to be ovulating regularly) and then suddenly have no bleeding (amenorrhea), let your doctor know, since this could be a sign of pregnancy. When amenorrhea occurs after *irregular* bleeding, you are not likely to be pregnant, since irregular bleeding is more common when you are not ovulating and therefore not releasing eggs that could be fertilized.

Other side effects that have been reported include acne, headaches, nausea, breast tenderness, dizziness, thinning of the hair on the head, and increased body hair. Some women will discontinue Norplant if they encounter one or more of these side effects; other women find they can deal with them, if they're not too severe, because the device is so effective at preventing unwanted pregnancies. Headaches, specifically migraines or other severe or persistent pain, should be reported to your doctor, especially if you also have any vision changes.

Norplant should not be inserted if you are pregnant.

It should also not be inserted if you have abnormal vaginal bleeding—until the cause is determined and you are treated, if necessary.

Certain medications may make Norplant less effective and increase the risk of unintended pregnancy. This effect is most clear with some antiseizure drugs taken for epilepsy and the antituberculosis medication rifampin. A connection is less well established for antibiotics. Be sure your doctor knows what drugs you are taking before deciding to use Norplant.

As far as anyone knows, the hormone in Norplant has no effect on a woman's sexual desire or on the act of intercourse—except possibly that it might increase your enjoyment because you don't have to worry about getting pregnant.

There is no known increase in any type of birth defects in babies born to women who got pregnant accidentally while using Norplant.

It is not yet known whether Norplant will have the same positive health effects as the Pill in terms of reducing the risk of endometrial (uterine lining) cancer and ovarian cancer, because this method has not been around long enough for the necessary data to be collected. Researchers familiar with the effects of hormones on the body think Norplant may turn out to be about as good as the Pill at reducing the risk of endometrial cancer (the Pill cuts risk about in half). They theorize that it probably will not be as good at reducing the risk of ovarian cancer as the Pill, because Norplant suppresses ovulation less consistently.

If you choose this method, be sure to read the package information carefully. Some of the information in it may sound quite scary. Your doctor, who knows your personal health history, can help you evaluate how potential risks might apply to you.

Who Is a Good Candidate for This Method

Women who think they've probably had all the children they want, but are not yet ready to take the irreversible step of surgical sterilization. Norplant can be an excellent option for such women. One thing to be aware of: Older women are more prone to irregular bleeding from a number of other causes, the most serious of which is uterine cancer. Since Norplant itself can cause irregular bleeding, this symptom needs to be carefully assessed in an older Norplant user. Often, but not always, abnormal bleeding will be heavier and crampier than one would expect from Norplant alone.

Young women, at the peak of their fertility, who need an extremely effective method of birth control.

Women who want a convenient option to taking a pill every day or who don't want the bother of a method that has to be used every time they have sex.

Women who are taking medicine for long periods of time that could harm a fetus if they got pregnant, as well as women who have medical conditions that could make a pregnancy dangerous. It might be an option for some HIV-positive women, depending on their symptoms and the medications they are taking. (Antituberculosis drugs, for example, can make Norplant less effective.) HIV-positive women should always use a condom to protect their sexual partners from the disease.

Who Is Not a Good Candidate for This Method

Women who can't take hormones (either because of a specific medical condition or because of the side effects they cause) will probably not be able to use this method. There are also other medical conditions that would probably rule out the use of Norplant, such as very high cholesterol and a history of a condition known as idiopathic intracranial hypertension (an increased pressure in the head from no apparent cause, which can cause headaches and blurred vision).

Norplant is unlikely to be the best choice for women who want to use a contraceptive to "space" their children—because it's a very expensive way to avoid pregnancy if used for less than about three years.

13

DEPO-PROVERA— "THE SHOT"

Currently Available

Depo-Provera (depot medroxyprogesterone acetate—or DMPA) is the only injectable contraceptive currently available in the United States. It was approved by the Food and Drug Administration (FDA) in 1992 and is made by the Upjohn Company.

Although many people in this country think of Depo-Provera as a "new" contraceptive, it has been used by more than 15 million women in ninety countries around the world for more than thirty years.

About 1 percent of the women in this country who use a reversible contraceptive currently choose Depo-Provera, according to Ortho's Annual Birth Control Studies. This is comparable to the number of women who choose IUDs (chapter 14) and Norplant (chapter 12).

What It Is

Depo-Provera is a synthetic progestin, a man-made hormone that is very similar to the natural progesterone that is made in a woman's ovaries. It comes in a slow-release, long-acting liquid form designed to be injected into muscle. Depo-Provera contains no estrogen.

Depo-Provera is available by prescription only. It should be prescribed only after a careful medical history and physical exam by a physician.

How It Works

A shot of Depo-Provera is given into the muscle of either the buttocks or the upper arm. The spot may be a bit sore for a day or two. In contrast to Norplant, no special training or equipment is needed to be able to administer this contraceptive. (The injection site should not be massaged when you get the shot or shortly afterward: This could cause the drug to disperse too quickly.)

Each injection provides extremely effective protection against pregnancy for three months. It is recommended that you get your first shot within five days of the start of a menstrual period. That way you are immediately protected and don't have to use another method of birth control while you're waiting for the shot to take full effect. From then on, as long as you're on time (within a week or two) for your next shot, you don't have to use a backup method after subsequent injections, either.

The progestin in Depo-Provera has several effects that work together to make pregnancy highly unlikely. One such effect is that it suppresses ovulation (the release of a mature egg from the ovary), at least partially and often completely. The fewer eggs your ovaries release, the fewer chances you have of getting pregnant. Progestins also make your cervical mucus thicker, so it's harder for sperm to get into the uterus and fallopian tubes, where they would normally fertilize an egg. Finally, progestins make the lining of the uterus thin and unreceptive to the implantation of an egg. Although Norplant and minipills work in essentially the same way, Depo-Provera uses a different type of progestin and there is a higher amount of the hormone circulating in the body.

How Effective It Is

Depo-Provera is one of the most effective reversible contraceptives available. Only about three out of every one thousand (0.3 percent) who use it get pregnant in a year, according to the package insert. As is also true of Norplant and IUDs, Depo-Provera's "typical" pregnancy rate is just as high as the "perfect use" pregnancy rate. That's because once you get your shot, you are continuously protected (unless of course you don't get your next one on time).

Just for comparison, about three typical Pill users out of every one hundred get pregnant in a year; and for every one hundred couples who use condoms, there are typically twelve pregnancies. If one hundred sexually active women used no method, you would expect about eighty-five of them to get pregnant in a year.

How Much It Costs

You will have to pay for the medicine itself (about $30 per dose; $120 per year just for the drug), plus the cost of a doctor's office visit—four times a year. If you are more than two weeks late for a shot, your doctor may want to do a pregnancy test for an additional charge.

Depo-Provera is covered by Medicaid in all fifty states.

Over time the cost averages out to be about the same as birth control pills and Norplant.

The Advantages of This Method

Ease of use is probably Depo-Provera's biggest draw. Once you've gotten a shot, you don't have to think about birth control again for three months. You don't have to take daily pills, you don't have to chart your temperature or cervical mucus, you don't have to put in a female condom, a cervical cap or diaphragm, and you don't have to have your partner put on a male condom (except of course to protect yourself against sexually transmitted diseases, if that's appropriate).

Depo-Provera's high effectiveness is another of its big advantages.

Some women who cannot take estrogens, because of the side effects they cause or because of medical contraindications, may be able to use Depo-Provera. (See "Safety and Side Effects," on page 162.)

After getting regular injections for about six months, about one in three women will have no bleeding at all, a condition called amenorrhea. After a year more than half of women will have no bleeding; after two years about three out of four. Amenorrhea does not hurt your body (it does not, for example, increase your risk of uterine cancer or other reproductive problems) and it does not mean the method is not working. Many women find that they like having no bleeding, as long as they have been told about this possibility beforehand and aren't worried that it means something is wrong.

Most women find they have less cramping and none of the midcycle pain that can accompany ovulation.

New mothers can use Depo-Provera. If you're not going to

nurse, you should get your first shot within five days of delivery. If you are going to breastfeed, the package insert suggests waiting until six weeks after the baby is born. Some doctors and family planning clinics feel it's safe to give the shot earlier, as soon as your milk production is well established. (In contrast you can't use the Pill until you stop nursing.) Clinical trials on nursing mothers have not shown any adverse effects on their babies, and progestins do not reduce milk flow as estrogen can.

Depo-Provera can also be given within five days of a pregnancy termination or miscarriage.

There is no time limit on how long you can continue to use Depo-Provera.

This contraceptive can be used without anyone—even your husband or boyfriend—knowing about it.

The Disadvantages of This Method

Once you get a shot, this method cannot be reversed for three months, until it wears off. (For more on this particular drawback, see "Reversibility," below.)

Irregular bleeding is common with this method. This is the most common reason women stop using Depo-Provera. In the first years of use irregular bleeding is about as frequent with Norplant as it is with Depo-Provera; as time goes on, more women on Depo start to have no periods at all (amenorrhea). In contrast, birth control pills that contain both estrogen and progesterone—which is the kind most women take—produce very regular, very light periods.

Weight gain has been reported in the literature to be more common in women who use Depo-Provera than the other progestin-only contraceptives. The package insert notes that about two-thirds of women gain five pounds the first year they use Depo-Provera and then continue to gain a bit each year after that. The increase appears to be in fat, as opposed to muscle or bone or water weight. Recently there has been some evidence that weight gain might not be as common as is generally thought.

It may be hard for some women to get to their doctors as often as four times a year for injections.

This method provides no protection against sexually transmitted diseases, including common infections such as chlamydia and gonorrhea, and the less common but deadly HIV, the virus that causes AIDS. However, women who take progestins are less prone to pelvic inflammatory disease (PID), an infection of the upper reproductive organs (uterus and tubes) that is a leading cause of female infertility. Experts think that the thickened cervical mucus helps to block disease-causing germs.

Reversibility

Once you get a shot, you can't change your mind about this form of contraception. There is no antidote, or medicine, that can negate the effects of Depo-Provera once it's in your body. You simply have to wait until the drug wears off. This will take at least three and a half months, possibly as long as six to eight months to be gone completely. There is really no good way to predict ahead of time whether you will like using this method—your past experiences (either good or bad) with other hormonal methods won't necessarily predict your response to this one.

If you wish to get pregnant after stopping Depo-Provera, there is no "waiting period"—you can start trying immediately. However, you should be aware that the average length of time it takes for a woman to get pregnant after her last dose wears off is about six months—meaning about ten months from her last shot. It can take even longer, particularly if you've been using this method for a long time, perhaps up to a year and a half. This is a significantly longer wait for fertility to return than you would have with Norplant or minipills or combined (estrogen-progestin) oral contraceptives.

Safety and Side Effects

Depo-Provera has proven very safe in numerous clinical studies conducted on millions of women over many years.

Since there is no estrogen in the shot, there is thought to be little or no increased risk of estrogen-related side effects that have been linked to Pill use, such as inflammation and blood clots in the veins (thrombophlebitis, thromboembolism). Therefore some women who cannot take estrogen may be able to use this or another progestin-only contraceptive.

However, to be on the safe side, the package insert warns that women who have a history of breast cancer, stroke, liver disease or tumors, or blood clots in the legs should not use this method of contraception. In some cases "possible" side effects are included in the package insert with little actual evidence that they occur in increased numbers in women who use this method. (The same is true of many drugs, including other prescription contraceptives.) If a problem is rare enough, it can be almost impossible to prove that it is *not* linked to the drug if someone happens to be taking it when the problem occurs. Studies to rule out every possible side effect would be exorbitantly expensive, extremely time-consuming, and in some cases impossible to carry out due to moral or ethical considerations.

If you think you might like to use Depo-Provera and you have a health problem that is more closely linked to estrogen than to progestins, talk to your doctor about it. Only someone who knows your personal health history can help you evaluate what the risks might be for you. If, for example, you had a clot in a leg vein following an injury (as opposed to one that formed spontaneously), your doctor might feel that taking progestins would pose only a small risk, if any; while the estrogen-plus-progestin in birth control pills might be a bigger risk.

There are fewer reported drug interactions with Depo-Provera than with either Norplant or oral contraceptives. Therefore some women who could not use the other hormonal methods because they took seizure medication or antibiotics, for example, may be able to use Depo-Provera. So far the only drug that has been shown to make Depo-Provera less effective is a cancer chemotherapy medicine called aminoglutethimide.

It is possible, but has not been conclusively shown in scientific studies, that Depo-Provera may be linked to a decrease in bone density, which could increase the risk of osteoporosis. This is an area that needs further study.

HDL (the "good") cholesterol is lowered in the blood of women using Depo-Provera, which may slightly increase the risk of heart disease.

There has been some concern about an association between Depo-Provera and cancer. This issue first came up many years ago during animal testing. Some of the dogs used in testing the drug developed breast cancers when they were given very high doses—twenty-five times the human amount. Ever since these early results scientists have been looking very carefully for any link to breast cancer in human beings. Several large, well-done studies have found no association overall. Some experts feel there may be a slightly increased risk in young women who use this method for a number of years. There is a similar possible association between breast cancer and oral contraceptives. At this point no one knows exactly how much the risk of breast cancer may be increased in young women, but—if in fact it is increased at all—the risk is probably quite small. (As for Norplant and minipills, there simply aren't enough data on these methods to know one way or the other.)

Also during early animal testing, some monkeys being given the drug developed endometrial cancer. Carefully conducted research by the World Health Organization, as well as Depo-Provera's subsequent use by millions of women around the world, has now made it clear that this does not happen in humans.

These two safety concerns were one of the main reasons the FDA took so long to approve Depo-Provera in this country. Experts at that agency are now convinced that this is a safe and effective method of contraception.

There are a number of minor side effects that are quite common. These can be bothersome but are not generally considered to be a health or safety concern. Weight gain and irregular bleeding are the most frequent. Other reported minor side effects include acne, nervousness, breast tenderness, dizziness, depression, hair loss, and fatigue.

Side effects aren't always bad. Depo-Provera does in fact have a number of positive "side effects." Because you bleed less overall (although possibly over more days), you are less likely to develop anemia. Women with sickle-cell disease have been shown to have fewer and less severe crises. Depo-Provera reduces the risk of endometrial cancer and may also make pelvic inflammatory disease (PID), premenstrual syndrome (PMS), and endometriosis less likely. Because of its high effectiveness, women using Depo-Provera are less likely to seek abortions than women using less reliable methods, and they are unlikely to face the risks of an unwanted pregnancy.

There is no evidence that Depo-Provera harms a fetus if you were to accidentally conceive while using it.

If you are thinking of using this method, be sure to read the package insert information. The package insert may be a bit intimidating. Your doctor can put the possible risks into perspective for you as an individual.

Who Is a Good Candidate for This Method

Older women who want a highly effective easy-to-use contraceptive but are not yet ready to take the permanent step of surgical sterilization.

Young, highly fertile women who want to be sure they don't get pregnant.

Any woman who finds it hard to remember to take a pill every day, or for whom it is difficult—for any reason—to consistently use a barrier method, such as condoms or a diaphragm.

Women who are not bothered by irregular bleeding patterns, once they understand why they occur and what to expect.

Women who have medical reasons that make it important that they not get pregnant. For example, women taking medications that can cause birth defects, or those who have a medical condition that would make a pregnancy dangerous.

Who Is Not a Good Candidate for This Method

Women who think they might be seriously bothered by irregular, unpredictable bleeding. Also women who would worry that they were pregnant every time they skipped a period will probably not be comfortable using this method.

Women who are, or might be, pregnant. While there is no

indication that the drug would harm a fetus, it is always considered safest not to expose pregnant women to any unnecessary medication.

Women who have unexplained abnormal vaginal bleeding. Since the drug itself can cause menstrual upsets, it would be hard to correctly diagnose and treat you—and know that the treatment has been successful—if you were given Depo-Provera. Older women are more prone to abnormal bleeding, for a number of reasons, including endometrial cancer.

Women who might want to get pregnant in the very near future. There is no way to reverse the effects of the shot once it is given, and it takes longer for fertility to return even after the shot wears off than it does for other progestin-only methods of contraception.

Women who would find it very difficult to get to the doctor's office every three months for a shot. (Note: It doesn't have to be *exactly* three months. If, for example, you're going on vacation the week your injection is due, you may be able to get it a week or two early or up to two weeks late.)

Women who hate getting shots.

Part Five

INTRAUTERINE DEVICES

CHAPTER

14

IUDs

Currently Available

ParaGard Cu-T 380 A (Ortho-McNeil Pharmaceutical)
Progestasert System (Alza Corporation)

IUDs are the choice of about one woman out of every one hundred using birth control today, according to the Ortho 1995 Annual Birth Control Study. That makes it about as popular as Norplant and Depo-Provera, and much less popular than the Pill or condoms. Around the world, on the other hand, IUDs are one of the most popular methods of birth control, used by as many as 20 to 30 percent of women in countries such as Germany and France.

You can get an IUD only by prescription. It must be inserted and removed by a doctor or trained health professional after a health history and physical exam has confirmed that this is an appropriate method of birth control for you.

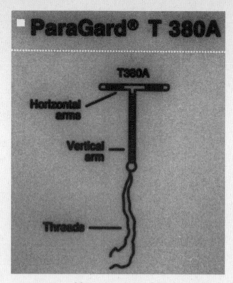

(Used by permission of Ortho-McNeil Pharmaceutical)

THE IUD

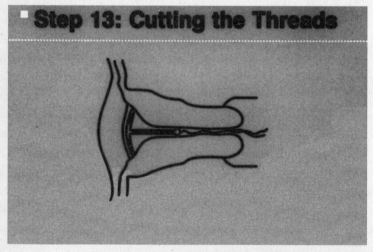

(Used by permission of Ortho-McNeil Pharmaceutical)

THE IUD IN THE UTERUS

What It Is

Both of the IUDs (or intrauterine devices) that are now available in the United States are T-shaped, and about 1½ inches long by 1¼ inches wide. The arms of the "T" are folded down inside a narrow plastic tube when the IUD is put in, then spring up into position once the inserter is removed.

Both IUDs are made of high-tech versions of plastic. The "active ingredient"—copper in the ParaGard, progesterone in the Progestasert—is either attached to this plastic frame or contained within it. Both types also have a "tail," a narrow, flexible plastic string that is attached to the bottom of the T and extends out through the cervical opening and into the upper vagina. A woman can feel for the tail to check that her IUD is still in place; and the tail is also used to remove the device.

How It Works

Surprisingly no one knows exactly how IUDs prevent pregnancy. It is probably a combination of factors, the result of both the IUD's active ingredient (copper or progesterone) and the physical presence of the device in the uterus, that work together to prevent fertilization. For example recent studies have shown that the IUD somehow interferes with sperm's ability to move and also makes the egg less easily fertilized—both in ways that are not entirely understood. The IUD also seems to cause an inflammatory response in the tissue lining the uterus, similar to what one would see in the case of an infection, although in this case not caused by the presence of germs. This appears to make the uterine lining less receptive to the implantation of a fertilized egg.

IUDs are usually inserted during the week after a menstrual period starts, to be sure you aren't pregnant. They can be inserted at any time if a pregnancy test is negative, or if you are using a very reliable method, such as Norplant or oral contraceptives, at the time. An IUD can be inserted as soon as the uterus returns to normal size after you have a baby or an abortion or miscarriage.

The insertion takes about fifteen minutes and is usually no more than mildly uncomfortable. For most women the discomfort will probably be about on a par with menstrual cramps. You will feel the pressure of the speculum holding your vagina open so that your doctor can see the cervix (the same feeling you have during any routine pelvic exam); you may feel a pinching sensation when your doctor grasps and steadies the cervix (the mouth of the uterus) with a device called a tenaculum; and you may have some twinges as first a "sound" (a measuring device) and, next, the IUD itself are gently threaded through the cervical opening and into the uterus. After the IUD is in place, you may have some cramping, and some people feel faint, so your doctor will probably ask you to rest quietly for a few minutes before you get up to go.

Since the IUD is put directly into the uterus, the possibility of infection is one of the biggest worries with an IUD insertion. Infections are most likely in the first weeks after insertion, and they can be serious—possibly causing permanent infertility. To keep the risk of infection as low as possible, an IUD should not be put in if you have any signs of infection or abnormal vaginal bleeding. Your doctor may want to run some lab tests and do a Pap smear ahead of time, just to be sure. (For more on the risk of infection, see "Disadvantages," on page 175.)

Once it's in place, a ParaGard can remain in place in your uterus for up to ten years. That's the longest of any reversible method of birth control. A Progestasert must be removed after one year.

How Effective It Is

IUDs are extremely good at what they do. Fewer than one woman in one hundred who uses a ParaGard will get pregnant during the first year the device is used. This is one of the lowest pregnancy rates of any reversible contraceptive. The progesterone IUD is a bit less effective: Approximately two out of every one hundred women who choose this method will get pregnant in a year. That's still quite good. Remember that, typically, three out of every one hundred Pill users get pregnant in a year; and about eighteen of every one hundred diaphragm users find themselves pregnant each year.

IUDs do not protect a woman against any type of sexually transmitted disease, including HIV, the virus that causes AIDS. If you are at risk for STDs, this is probably not the best birth control option for you.

How Much It Costs

The ParaGard, which is used by the vast majority of the women using an IUD today, costs about $200. The total cost for a visit to your doctor's office or clinic for insertion, checkups, and removal will vary, but will likely add up to at least several hundred dollars. This sounds like a lot of money, but since the ParaGard can be left in place for up to ten years, it is actually one of the most cost-effective means of birth control available. (Progestasert, because it must be replaced yearly, is not nearly as cost-effective.)

The Advantages of This Method

The IUD is highly effective, inexpensive when the cost is averaged out over time, and easy to use. Studies have shown that 98 percent of users are happy with their IUDs, one of the highest ratings of all methods. More than half of the women who now have an IUD have had one before.

The ParaGard can be used for up to ten years. That's the longest a woman will be protected by any method short of surgical sterilization.

Progestasert, the hormone-containing IUD, significantly reduces menstrual bleeding and cramps. However, since this type of IUD must be replaced every year (and infection is most likely shortly after insertion), many health care providers only use a Progestasert if there is a specific reason you can't tolerate a ParaGard—if, for example, you have very heavy, crampy periods or if you are allergic to copper.

An IUD is one of the most hassle-free contraceptives available. Once inserted, you can basically forget about it. You don't have to plan ahead, or go fumbling around for a condom or your diaphragm every time you want to have sex, or remember to take a pill every day. During sex you and your partner won't even know the IUD is there. (Occasionally men report that they can feel the tail of the IUD, most often soon after insertion. If this minor annoyance persists, sometimes the string can be cut shorter.) The only thing you have to remember is to check for the string at least once a month after your period to be sure the IUD hasn't come out—either entirely (in which case you'd feel nothing) or partially (in which case you would feel the string and the hard end of the IUD itself protruding through the cervical opening).

The Disadvantages of This Method

The IUD provides no protection against sexually transmitted diseases, so anyone who's at risk needs to use another method (condoms are best) either instead of or in addition to the IUD. A woman is considered at risk for STDs if she has sex with more than one partner, or if her partner has sex with others.

The ParaGard can increase menstrual bleeding, spotting, and cramping, although for most women not enough to be bothersome. About 10 to 15 percent of women who try an IUD will end up having it taken out because they consider the changes in their menstrual cycles to be a significant problem.

As mentioned above, IUDs do sometimes (2 to 10 percent of the time) come out by themselves, usually within the first three months after insertion. Expulsion is more common in younger women and in those who have heavy, crampy periods. Your risk of pregnancy is increased when an IUD is partially expelled.

Probably the most serious problem associated with IUDs is an increased risk of PID, or pelvic inflammatory disease. This infection can be dangerous, and in rare cases can necessitate a hysterectomy or even cause death. Today such serious complications are quite uncommon.

Twenty years ago, however, there were serious problems with IUDs, for at least two reasons: First, IUDs were given to women who would not be considered good candidates for this type of contraception today—for example, because they were at high risk for sexually transmitted diseases. Second, there was one particularly problematic type of IUD available, called the Dalkon Shield. Although many women used the crab-shaped Dalkon Shield for years with no ill effects, it was taken off the market in 1975 in the wake of lawsuits brought against its manufacturer by thousands of women.

Current IUDs are smaller, shaped to fit more easily in the uterus, and have a single-fiber ("mono filament") tail, instead of the multistrand tail, used on the Dalkon Shield, that "wicked" germs from the vagina into the uterus. IUDs are now more effective as well: Some of the most serious problems with earlier IUDs occurred when women got pregnant with the devices in place. (In addition, pregnancy tests were not as sensitive or widely available when the early IUDs came out, so when a pregnancy did occur, it was generally diagnosed later, making removal of the device that much more difficult.)

Negative perception of the IUD persists in this country even today, among both women and health care providers. There are now many carefully done scientific studies showing that the ParaGard has a very low infection rate, only slightly higher than that in women who don't use IUDs. Certainly you should not choose an IUD if you're at risk for pelvic infection or other complications, but if this method is a good choice, you also shouldn't be afraid to use it based on outdated facts. All forms of birth control are associated with risks—for example allergic reactions to spermicides and latex condoms, blood clots with the Pill, and with most methods there's a significantly higher pregnancy rate.

Reversibility

Most women quickly become fertile again after an IUD is removed. Pregnancy rates are about the same for past IUD users as they are for women of the same age who have never used an IUD. One large and well-designed study (the Oxford Family Planning Study) found no delayed return to fertility in IUD users.

Safety and Side Effects

You will probably be given a pregnancy test before an IUD is inserted, unless you and your doctor are quite sure you are not pregnant. If you are pregnant, the IUD should not be inserted.

You (and ideally your sexual partner, too) should be evaluated for STDs, and treated, if necessary, before an IUD is put in. STDs often have no visible symptoms.

The risk of pelvic infection is highest in the first month after insertion. For this reason some doctors will prescribe antibiotics for you to take afterward, on a just-in-case basis. However, scientific studies haven't shown that this actually reduces the risk of pelvic infection. The signs of infection include fever, chills, pain or tenderness in the lower belly, pain during sex, and abnormal vaginal discharge. Call your doctor right away if you have signs of infection.

Pregnancy with an IUD in place is highly unlikely. However, if you do have an IUD and miss a period, it's important to find out why as soon as possible. If you are in the early stages of pregnancy, the IUD can usually be removed quickly and easily. As the pregnancy advances, the uterus expands and the tail of the IUD is often pulled up into the uterus, making it more difficult to remove the device. If the IUD is left in place, the risk of early miscarriage is about 40 percent. If the pregnancy continues, there is a risk of a potentially life-threatening septic abortion—a miscarriage complicated by infection. Women who continue a pregnancy with an IUD in place also have a higher risk of premature delivery. Anyone who wishes to continue a pregnancy with an IUD in place must understand these risks and be followed very carefully by her doctor.

Another reason for early diagnosis of a missed period is the possibility of an ectopic, or tubal, pregnancy. IUDs (particularly progesterone-containing IUDs) prevent ectopic pregnancies slightly less well than they do normal uterine pregnancies. An ectopic pregnancy can be life-threatening and must be treated (by either medical or surgical means) as soon as possible.

You will probably be given detailed written information describing this method's risks and benefits, which you will be asked to read, and possibly sign, before an IUD is inserted. This is done in part to protect IUD manufacturers, because of this method's past history of litigation. The form is quite technical and can also be quite frightening to read—it spells out every possible problem in excruciating detail. It is important that you talk over any fears or concerns with your doctor before you go ahead and have the IUD inserted.

Who Is a Good Candidate for This Method

The ideal candidate for this method has one sexual partner and one or more children. Not surprisingly the vast majority of IUD users are in their thirties and forties. Younger women who have never had children can sometimes use this method safely, but they need to consider their options carefully before doing so. Both the pregnancy rate and the incidence of problems (bleeding, expulsion) are somewhat higher in this group, and young women may be more likely to have multiple partners, which increases the risk of STD infection.

Women who want high effectiveness from their birth control method. IUD users don't want to get pregnant accidentally. This is not an insignificant factor, considering that surveys have shown that almost half of all pregnancies in this country today are "unintended"—and *over 40 percent of those pregnancies* occurred in women who were using some form of birth control at the time. Many women have turned to an IUD (or another low-maintenance method, such as Depo-Provera or Norplant) after a "contraceptive failure" because their birth control was simply too difficult for them to use consistently and correctly. For women with hectic lives and irregular hours, and for those who travel frequently, even remembering to take a pill at the same time every day can be a challenge.

The ParaGard IUD can be a good option for women who want a highly effective method but can't use oral contraceptives or other methods containing hormones for medical reasons (high blood pressure, a history of blood clots), if you tend to forget to take pills, or if you were bothered by significant side effects from hormones, such as bloating, nausea, or migraines.

Who Is Not a Good Candidate for This Method

Women who have sex with more than one man (or who have a partner who has sex with others), since they are more likely to get a sexually transmitted disease. This method does not provide protection against STDs and may increase the risk of pelvic inflammatory disease (or PID, a possible consequence of infection that can cause infertility), particularly if you have an STD when the IUD is put in. Women who have had a sexually transmitted disease or PID should be very cautious about choosing this method of birth control.

Women who have had problems with an IUD in the past (heavy bleeding, infection, multiple expulsions) should probably choose a different method.

Women who have fibroids (benign tumors of the uterus) large enough to distort the uterine cavity should probably choose a different method.

Women who have never given birth. IUDs are marketed primarily for women who have had children. Sometimes this method can be a good choice for a woman who hasn't carried a baby to term, although it is somewhat more likely to be expelled and more likely to increase bleeding and cramping, probably due to the fact that the uterus is smaller in women who have not had children.

Young, single women, who are likely to have more than one sex partner over time. This puts them at risk for PID, and raises the possibility that they might not be able to have children later in life if they want to.

Women who have health problems that reduce the body's ability to fight infection. This would include those who take steroids for rheumatoid arthritis or colitis, for example, and anyone who is HIV positive.

Part Six

STERILIZATION

TUBAL LIGATION

Currently Available

Although you generally hear very little about it, tubal ligation is a hugely popular form of birth control. For several years now sterilization (both male and female combined) has been running neck and neck with the Pill in popularity, each chosen by about one in four couples. About 15 percent of all women of childbearing age have been sterilized. Not surprisingly the women who choose this method are typically over thirty, married, and have two or more children, according to the Ortho 1995 Annual Birth Control Study.

What It Is

Tubal ligation is surgery done to permanently close (cut and/or block off) a woman's fallopian tubes so that sperm and egg can no longer meet. There are two fallopian tubes, each connecting an ovary to the uterus. After the tubes are closed off, the egg and sperm simply dissolve when they reach the blocked area of the tubes.

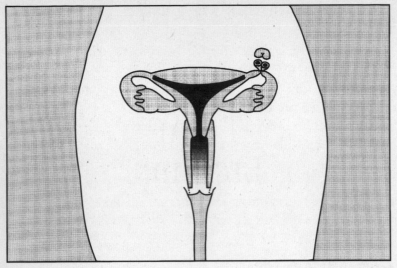

(AVSC International)

Cutting and tying the tubes

TUBAL LIGATION

Tubal ligation does not involve removing any organs: It is not a hysterectomy, and it does not, as some women worry, cause menopause. After the surgery you will continue to have periods, and sex will feel just like it did before—except that you won't have to worry about an accidental pregnancy. Except for one or two small scars (which fade over time, sometimes becoming almost invisible) no one would be able to tell from looking at you or from having sex with you that you have had this operation.

How It Works

Tubal ligation can be done in a hospital, clinic, or out-patient ("same-day") surgery center. Today no matter what type of anesthesia is used (general, spinal or epidural, even local combined with drugs to help you relax), most women will be able to go home the same day they have surgery. You can have the operation while you're in the hospital to deliver a baby, or at any other time unrelated to pregnancy or delivery. In this country the surgery itself is most often performed by obstetrician-gynecologists. As with any type of surgery, experience counts: Doctors who have done a lot of tubal ligations tend to have the highest success rates and the fewest complications.

Tubal ligation can be done in a variety of ways. There are differences both in how the doctor gets to the tubes and in how the tubes are sealed closed. Your doctor will use the technique he or she feels works best and has the most experience with. Blocking the tubes can be accomplished by electrocautery (burning with an electric device), by tying them with suture material, or by closing them off with one of several types of clips or rings.

Today the most common way to reach the tubes in this country is laparoscopy. This type of operation is often referred to as "Band-Aid" surgery because it requires only one or two small incisions in the lower abdomen—incisions small enough to be covered by a simple Band-Aid. The laparoscope is a long, narrow viewing instrument, a bit like a miniature periscope. It is inserted into the abdomen through an incision near the belly button so that the doctor can see the tubes. To separate the internal organs and make it easier for the doctor to see, a harmless gas, usually carbon dioxide, is first pumped into the belly through a needle. Then the small instruments that are used to actually clasp and block the tubes are carefully inserted into the abdomen—either through the same incision or through a second small incision near the pubic-hair line.

Tubal ligation by laparoscopy normally takes about half an hour. After the procedure your doctor will want you to rest at the hospital or clinic for several hours before you go home. Your doctor will then give you specific instructions about how soon you can resume normal activities (normally in about three to four days) and sex (probably as soon as you feel up to it). Before you leave after surgery, you should also know what types of side effects are normal and expected after laparoscopy and which should prompt a call to your doctor. (See "Safety and Side Effects," on page 190.)

Another common "same-day" sterilization technique is the minilaparotomy. This approach can be used either postpartum or at any time unrelated to pregnancy or delivery. In this type of surgery the doctor reaches the tubes by way of an incision in the lower abdomen, just above the pubic bone, and low enough that the scar will be hidden by your pubic hair. If the procedure is done within a few days after a woman has a baby, the incision is placed below the belly button instead of near the pubic hair, since the uterus and tubes are higher in the belly at this time.

The minilaparotomy is about equal in safety and effectiveness to a laparoscopy, and it doesn't require as much high-tech equipment. Because minilaparotomy involves a larger incision, recovery is likely to be more painful and take somewhat longer. Minilaparotomy may not be the best choice if a woman is overweight; and it can be hard to move the tubes so they can be closed off through the small incision if her uterus and tubes are held in place by scar tissue (from previous surgery, infection, endometriosis). Minilaparotomy is the technique of choice for sterilizations done immediately after delivery.

An even larger incision, called a laparotomy, is used when a sterilization is done at the same time as the C-section delivery of a baby or some other abdominal surgery that requires more access to the pelvis. This larger incision will be more painful after surgery and require a longer recovery period.

There are also some much less common approaches to sterilization—through the vagina, for example. These techniques may have been developed originally to try to avoid an external scar, although there's less incentive to go this route now that laparoscopy (with its tiny incisions) has become more widely available. Also, some studies have shown that infection may be more common in vaginal sterilizations than for either laparoscopy or minilaparotomy.

How Effective It Is

Tubal ligation is one of the most effective—if not the most effective—birth control method available. Fewer than one woman in two hundred (0.4 percent) becomes pregnant in the first year after tubal ligation. If that number is higher than you might expect, it's because a significant percentage of what experts must count as "failures" are women who were already pregnant, but didn't know it, when they had the procedure. True failures, in which the severed ends of the tubes manage to reconnect, or the wrong structure (a ligament, for example, instead of a fallopian tube) was severed, or the closing off of the tube was incomplete, are uncommon. Studies have shown that postpartum tubal ligation has pregnancy rates slightly higher than those done at other times, possibly due to the fact that tubes are more swollen and harder to close off immediately after you have a baby. It doesn't seem to make much difference, in terms of effectiveness, which method (cautery, clips, rings) is used to close off the tubes.

Tubal ligation provides no protection against sexually transmitted diseases, including HIV, the virus that causes AIDS. If you or your partner are at risk for infection, one of you should use a condom.

How Much It Costs

Although prices vary from doctor to doctor and from one part of the country to another, tubal ligation by a private doctor will probably cost two thousand dollars or more. If it is available at a family planning clinic such as Planned Parenthood, the cost may be significantly lower. Local anesthesia and same-day surgery should cost less than general anesthesia and overnight hospital stays. Your health insurance may cover at least part of the cost.

Although this method is expensive at first, you never have to spend another penny on birth control after a tubal ligation. The longer you have it, then, the more economical it becomes.

Vasectomy for a man is much less expensive (and safer) than tubal ligation.

The Advantages of This Method

Tubal ligation is effective immediately. As soon as the tubes are closed off, fertilization can no longer occur.

After the surgery you will be free to enjoy sex, and any children you already have, without having to worry about an accidental pregnancy.

You don't have to bother with, or worry about, birth control anymore. No more pills, no more diaphragm and jelly, no more condoms (unless of course you need STD protection).

The Disadvantages of This Method

Tubal ligation is surgery. Although the operation is generally quite safe, there are always some risks involved. (See "Safety and Side Effects.")

This method must be considered irreversible. There are women who regret having had the operation. Most often this applies to younger women, or to those whose lives change in ways they could not anticipate (they remarry, or have a child who dies).

Although tubal ligation is cost-effective over the years, the surgery must be paid for up front. Tubal ligation is more expensive than vasectomy.

Tubal ligation does not provide any protection against common sexually transmitted diseases, such as herpes and chlamydia. It also provides no protection against the transmission of the HIV virus, which causes AIDS.

Reversibility

Surgical sterilization should be considered irreversible. You should only choose this method if you are sure you do not want to have any more children. This is not a step to be taken lightly. If you are considering a tubal ligation with the idea of reversal in the back of your mind, it is probably best to wait until you are sure this decision is right for you.

That said, it must be noted that reversal is sometimes possible and that success rates have improved a great deal in recent years. However, reconnecting the tubes is major surgery. It is much more complicated, more risky, and much more costly than severing the tubes in the first place. It also requires great skill on the part of the surgeon. Even if the tubes can be successfully reattached, a successful pregnancy does not automatically follow.

How the tubes were blocked during the sterilization procedure makes a difference in how likely reversal is to be successful. Electrocautery, for example, tends to destroy much more of the tubes than do rings. The more undamaged tube the surgeon has to work with, the greater your odds of successful reattachment.

In some cases in-vitro fertilization may be an option after sterilization: IVF involves removing eggs from the ovaries, fertilizing them outside the body, then returning several embryos to the uterus—thus bypassing the tubes. Although it may sound simple enough, IVF is expensive and can be a grueling process to undergo.

Safety and Side Effects

Major complications from tubal ligation are uncommon. However, surgery is never without risks.

Anesthesia used during surgery is one possible source of complications. General anesthesia, although normally very safe these days, has more potential for problems (including death) than does local or spinal/epidural anesthesia. It also requires more high-tech equipment and trained personnel to administer and monitor. General anesthesia is the most common choice in this country for sterilizations.

During the surgery internal organs may be injured accidentally—cut or punctured by an instrument, for example, or burned by the electrocautery device. Here is where the skill and experience of your surgeon can make a big difference. Deaths, while very uncommon, have occurred from the piercing of a major abdominal blood vessel during surgery. Another rare but potentially lethal occurrence is carbon dioxide embolism during laparoscopy—in which a bubble of gas gets into a blood vessel and travels to a vital organ, such as the heart or lungs.

Infection is always a possibility after surgery. Your doctor will give you instructions for caring for the skin incisions. You will also be told the signs and symptoms to be alert for (such as fever, abdominal pain or swelling, fainting, nausea, vomiting) that might signal an infection or another internal problem, such as bleeding.

You will be given instructions about how long to take it easy, when you can start having sex again, what aches and pains are normal, and which should prompt a call. After laparoscopy you may feel gas pains in unexpected places—such as the shoulders—which could last several days. This is not dangerous, but it can be uncomfortable, and possibly frightening if you weren't warned about it ahead of time. Usually you will need to take it easy for at least a few days, and avoid lifting heavy things or doing hard work for a week or more. After a week most women are feeling pretty much back to normal.

After the surgery, and for reasons that are not well understood, some women's periods become heavy and irregular. This usually happens over time, not right away, so there has been an ongoing debate about whether this phenomenon is actually related to the surgery, or if it would have occurred anyway. (Irregular periods are quite common as women approach menopause.) There is speculation that, if there is indeed a connection, the irregular bleeding might be caused by some type of injury to the ovary or its blood supply during surgery. If you have had a tubal ligation and start to have heavy or irregular menstrual bleeding, discuss it with your doctor. He or she may want to run a few diagnostic tests, just to rule out other problems that can have similar symptoms.

Some experts believe that minilaparotomy tends to be more painful than laparoscopy and that recovery takes longer. Also, possible complications such as bladder injury, bleeding, and infection are higher than for laparoscopy. On the other hand the risk of rare but deadly air embolism is entirely avoided with minilaparotomy, since no gas is pumped into the abdomen.

Who Is a Good Candidate for This Method

Women who are sure they do not want to have any more children.

Women whose age or medical problems could make a pregnancy physically risky.

Who Is Not a Good Candidate for This Method

Anyone who is not absolutely sure she's ready to choose an irreversible method of birth control. You should never feel pressured to make this decision—by a doctor, partner, family member, or anyone else. Only you can decide if tubal ligation is right for you.

If you are not completely comfortable with the idea of this permanent step, a long-acting, highly effective method such as Norplant or Depo-Provera or an IUD might be a good alternative, at least for the time being. You can always opt for sterilization in the future, if and when you feel ready.

16

VASECTOMY

Currently Available

Sterilization is currently the second most commonly used method of birth control in this country, chosen by about one in four couples (24 percent, to be precise, according to the Ortho 1995 Annual Birth Control Study). About 10 percent of men of reproductive age have had a vasectomy. The couples who are most likely to choose this method are over thirty, married, and already have two or more children.

One reason the numbers are so large for sterilization is that it's permanent. As more men and women choose this method each year, their numbers are added to those who have already chosen it, so the total number of users increases. For reversible methods, such as the Pill, on the other hand, some women will start using it, others will switch to a different method, so the number of users tends to stay more stable over time. Right now there is also a large crop of baby boomers who are currently in the age range (midthirties and older) at which couples tend to choose sterilization.

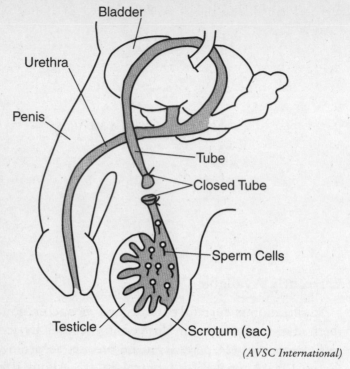

(*AVSC International*)

VASECTOMY

What It Is

A minor surgical procedure designed to prevent sperm from getting into the semen, the fluid that is released when a man ejaculates.

How It Works

Vasectomy involves cutting the vas deferens, the narrow tubes through which sperm travel from the testicles, where they are manufactured, to the penis. This surgery is most often performed by a urologist in his office or at an outpatient surgery center.

Except for the absence of sperm, the semen remains exactly the same after a vasectomy. Since sperm are only a small part of the semen (it also contains fluid from other glands that serve as nutrients for the sperm), it is impossible to tell with the naked eye that a man has had a vasectomy. Sex hormones produced by the testicles remain untouched by the procedure. Likewise sexual desire, arousal, erections, and orgasm are not physically affected in any way by a vasectomy. (Psychological fallout can sometimes cause problems, however; see "Safety and Side Effects," on page 198.)

The surgery itself is very safe and can take as little as fifteen minutes. Only local anesthesia is needed. Before the surgery the hair around the penis will be clipped short, and the entire genital area will be carefully cleaned with antiseptic solution. The doctor can carry out the actual procedure in one of several different ways. To reach the vas, he may make either a single small incision in the middle of the scrotum (the hair-covered sac that holds the testicles), just below the base of the penis; or he may make two small incisions, one on each side. There is also a "no-scalpel" vasectomy, which involves using specially designed instruments, instead of a scalpel, to puncture a small hole in the scrotal skin and grasp and sever the vas. No-scalpel vasectomies are currently done by a limited number of doctors in this country.

Most often a surgeon will not simply cut the vas deferens but will remove a piece of each one, increasing the odds that the tubes will not reconnect as they heal. One or both of the severed ends will be closed off, using one of several techniques (such as tying them with suture thread or sealing them with an electro-cautery device). The small incisions in the scrotum may either be closed with a stitch or left to heal on their own.

Immediately after the operation a man will rest for perhaps

a half hour and then be allowed to go home. Once he is at home, it is important that he follow his doctor's instructions to reduce the risk of any complications. He may be advised to use an ice pack on the area for several hours the first day and to take it easy for two or more days. Heavy lifting, bike riding, running, or any other activity that strains the groin area should be avoided for about a week.

Sex will probably be okayed after about two or three days, or as soon after that as the man feels comfortable. A couple must use another form of contraception until the doctor has confirmed that all the sperm that were already in the man's reproductive system at the time of surgery have been expelled from the body. This can take a number of weeks, even months, depending on how often he has sex.

How Effective It Is

Vasectomy is extremely dependable. True failures (in which the severed tubes manage to reconnect as they heal) are rare—less than one in two hundred. Most "failures" occur within the first weeks after the procedure and are due to sperm that were already in the reproductive tract.

How Much It Costs

This method must be paid for up front. Vasectomy may cost as little as $250 if performed in a family planning clinic such as Planned Parenthood, or as much as $1,000 if done by a private physician. The price varies in different areas of the country. Check with your insurance company to see if some or all of the cost is covered.

Averaged out over time, vasectomy is one of the most cost-effective methods of birth control available.

The Advantages of This Method

Vasectomy can be very freeing to a couple. After it's done, you don't have to fuss with birth control or worry about an unplanned pregnancy.

Unbeatable effectiveness is another of vasectomy's top draws.

The procedure itself is very safe and simple, as operations go, and quite quick. It is less risky than tubal ligation for a woman.

Vasectomy is inexpensive when the cost is averaged out over a number of years. It is also much less expensive than tubal ligation.

The Disadvantages of This Method

The fact that the procedure is irreversible is this method's biggest disadvantage. When facing unanticipated changes in their lives (such as the death of a child or a remarriage), some people may regret having chosen sterilization. Young men in particular should consider this step very carefully before they decide to undergo the procedure. Be sure you are convinced that this is something you want to do, not something you're doing to please someone else. (Although a sperm sample can be frozen before a vasectomy, just in case of a change of heart, not all sperm freeze well, and pregnancy rates are not as high as with fresh sperm.)

This method involves surgery that, although minor, does need to be done under proper sterile conditions and by a trained physician.

Unlike female sterilization, which is effective immediately, it can take months before a couple can have sex without using a backup contraceptive. It's not safe to stop using the backup until a doctor has confirmed that there are no more live sperm in the man's ejaculate.

Vasectomy provides no protection against sexually transmitted diseases, including HIV and AIDS. If you or your partner is at risk of infection, one of you should use a condom.

This method renders a man sterile but will not, of course, protect his partner from pregnancy if she has sex with someone else.

Reversibility

A man should only have a vasectomy if he considers it to be a permanent step. Reattaching the vas deferens is possible in some cases, although the surgery is much more complicated and expensive than the original vasectomy. Even if the tubes are successfully reconnected and even if sperm can be detected in the ejaculate, sometimes those sperm may not be capable of fertilizing an egg. Doctors do not know exactly why this happens, but it may be related to sperm antibodies. (See "Safety and Side Effects," below.)

Safety and Side Effects

As long as it is done in sterile conditions, by a doctor who is experienced in the technique, vasectomy is extremely safe. Typical aftereffects of surgery are usually no more than temporary bruising and tenderness. The area should be kept clean and dry for several days to reduce the risk of infection.

Occasionally a lump called a granuloma will form at the blocked end of the vas. The lump will almost always go away by itself; but if it doesn't, or if it gets infected, it may need to be drained. Bleeding, which can result in a blood clot or bruise called a hematoma, is another possible aftereffect, although this, too, is not very common. To reduce this risk, strenuous activity should be avoided for about a week. In rare cases a large hematoma or an infection could require the removal of a testicle. Another possible but not common after-effect of surgery is a condition called epididymitis, an inflammation of a small gland on the testicle where the sperm are stored. Epididymitis usually goes away by itself, although antibiotics may be required if infection is the cause.

If a man suspects any problems, or has any questions about what's normal and what's not after a vasectomy, he should call his doctor. He should let the doctor know immediately if he runs a fever, notices pus or bleeding, or has a lot of discomfort or swelling.

There are few permanent side effects of vasectomy. Most men who have had this done will develop sperm antibodies, substances in the blood that reduce the activity of sperm. Studies looking into this phenomenon have uncovered no problems or negative impact on a man's health from sperm antibodies, although it's possible that they may be linked to infertility after a reversal operation. Some men who have not had vasectomies also develop sperm antibodies.

In research done a number of years ago monkeys that had vasectomies and were fed a high-fat diet seemed to be more likely to develop heart disease. Since then extensive data have been collected on many thousands of men who have had this procedure. The conclusion: There is no indication of an increased risk of heart disease after vasectomy in humans.

More recently there has been the suggestion of a link between prostate cancer and vasectomy. At the moment men are left a bit up in the air on this issue. In 1993 the National Institutes of Health held a special conference for top experts to review all of the best and latest scientific studies available. That panel of experts concluded that the evidence was too weak and too conflicting to merit any cautions about the safety of vasectomy. They did not even feel it was necessary to recommend that men who had vasectomies be screened more frequently for prostate cancer. Close scrutiny on this topic is sure to continue, however, and men who have had a vasectomy or are considering getting one should be alert for further developments.

What they say about sex being 90 percent in your head is true: Although there may be no organic reason for it, a man who worries about his sexual performance or who feels literally "impotent" after the procedure could end up developing sexual problems. The idea of permanent sterility can sometimes be harder to handle than men anticipate. The best approach is to get counseling and ask all your questions before you have the procedure. If this feeling only hits after surgery, counseling at that time may be in order.

Who Is a Good Candidate for This Method

Men who are sure they do not want to be the biological father of any children in the future.

Men who can be comfortable separating literal "sterility" from their ability as good lovers and partners.

Who Is Not a Good Candidate for This Method

Men who might want to be the biological father of a child in the future.

Men who can't stand the thought of the surgery, particularly in this sensitive area.

Men who are worried that the procedure might affect their masculinity or sexuality. There is no scientific evidence that it does, although mental fears, if not addressed, can end up affecting physical performance.

Part Seven

CONTRACEPTIVE FAILURE

WHEN BIRTH CONTROL FAILS

Why Birth Control Fails

More than 6 million women in this country become pregnant each year. According to studies by the Alan Guttmacher Institute and others, more than half (57 percent) of those pregnancies are unintended, accidental. More than 40 percent of the women who find themselves in this position were using some type of birth control at the time.

If, instead of looking at all women over a year's time, you took a group of women and followed them through the years, another startling statistic emerges: About 74 percent of women—*almost three out of four*—will have an unintended pregnancy at some point during their reproductive years. Not all "accidental" pregnancies are unwanted, of course. Sometimes, for example, a couple might simply have been putting off having a baby for a while, or trying to make up their minds about whether to have another, and be perfectly happy when the "decision" is made for them.

Clearly, accidental pregnancy is a common occurrence. Yet

in spite of the statistics, this is a subject that most of us would rather push to the back of our minds. After all, you're careful, right? And even though a lot of other people get pregnant by accident, it's not going to happen to you. Right?

The problem is, no matter how careful you are, you can still get pregnant by mistake. The failure rates of various contraceptives were discussed at the beginning of this book (see page 12) but some things bear repeating: You can use a condom every time, you can always put in your diaphragm, you can take your pill every night after you brush your teeth, and you can still get pregnant. Because even if you were perfect, the contraceptives themselves aren't. Some methods do come fairly close to perfect protection, but even with Norplant or Depo-Provera or the ParaGard IUD, pregnancies do occur.

And that's only considering using birth control under ideal conditions—exactly right, every time. In real life, as we all know, things are rarely that simple. You go to your boyfriend's apartment after the movies, but your diaphragm is in the bedside table next to your bed. Or you go on vacation and forget to pack your birth control pills. Or you do remember to pack your pills, but they're in the bag the airline sent to San Francisco instead of San Juan. These things happen. And because they do, the typical pregnancy rates for many contraceptives are considerably higher than the theoretical ideal.

Home Pregnancy Tests

Your period is late. Just a few days late, but late just the same. Are you actually pregnant, or did something—stress? that crazy diet you've been on?—just throw your menstrual cycle out of whack? Women today have a significant advantage when it comes to being able to answer this question: home pregnancy tests.

Today's home pregnancy tests are quite accurate. They can detect a pregnancy very early, around the time you miss your first period. (Remember, by the time you skip a period, you are probably about two weeks pregnant.) In fact the over-the-counter tests may in some cases be almost identical to the urine testing done by commercial and clinic labs. Home pregnancy tests are also easy to get when you need them (at most drugstores and supermarkets), and can give you results in a matter of minutes. In most cases they are quite simple to do, if you read and follow the instructions carefully. Manufacturers keep trying to make the kits simpler, so it's harder to make mistakes. They are not even very expensive (probably about fifteen dollars, depending on the particular brand you choose and where you get it), considering that what you're buying is convenience and privacy.

What Are Your Options?

There are basically four things you can do if you're faced with the possibility of an unintended pregnancy:

- Emergency after-the-fact contraception, the "morning-after pill." This method only works if used within three days (seventy-two hours) of unprotected sex, so it is only useful in certain situations—if, for example, the condom breaks. By the time a home pregnancy test turns positive, it's too late for this option.

- Surgical pregnancy termination, or abortion.

- Medical pregnancy termination—in which drugs are used, instead of surgery, to end the pregnancy.

- Continuation of the pregnancy.

THE MORNING-AFTER PILL

Oral contraceptives taken at the right time and in the right way have been used for years in this country at many family planning clinics, at rape treatment centers, and by some private physicians as a "morning-after" emergency contraceptive. This is not a method you should rely on or use frequently. It should be reserved for emergencies only.

The Pill is not officially sanctioned for this use. There is no mention of it on the current FDA-approved labeling that comes with oral contraceptives. (It is, however, approved and widely available in countries such as England and the Netherlands, and also in South America, Africa, and Asia.) Although the Pill is not FDA approved for this use, it is legal for doctors to prescribe it to be used in this way. Physicians do this often, and with many different types of medication, in what is known as an off-label use.

For the morning-after pill to work, it must be given within seventy-two hours of unprotected intercourse. Several different brands of pills can be used, but they must be given in the right number and at the right time. What's often referred to as the Yuzpe regimen is as follows: Two Ovral tablets (or four Lo/Ovral tablets) less than seventy-two hours after unprotected sex; followed by two (or four) more of the same twelve hours later.

Do not borrow birth control pills from a friend and try to do this on your own. You must consult your doctor or go to a family planning clinic to be sure (a) that the treatment is necessary in your particular situation; and (b) that the pills in this dosage are safe for you to use. Women who can't use birth control pills for medical reasons should not use them for emergency contraception. Nausea and vomiting are common from the high dose of estrogen.

Studies have shown that morning-after pills are effective more than 90 percent of the time. Normally you will start to bleed within two weeks after taking the pills. Your doctor will discuss what can be done if bleeding doesn't occur in that time. If you skip a menstrual period, a pregnancy test should be done.

The estrogen in the pills affects the lining of the uterus so that the fertilized egg, if there is one, cannot implant. The morning-after pills will not work if the egg has already implanted—if, for example, the pills are taken too late or you were already pregnant, without knowing it, before the condom broke.

It is hard to know whether the morning-after pill will ever be officially approved for widespread use in this country. There is now quite a bit of evidence, both from the United States and elsewhere in the world, that this is a safe and effective way to reduce the risk of an unwanted pregnancy. If a drug company did apply for this use to be listed on the labels, the FDA might approve it. However, there is little economic incentive for a major drug company to push for the labeling change. And there is much in this country's current political climate to dissuade them from trying.

THE "MORNING-AFTER" IUD

An intrauterine device can also be an effective form of emergency, after-the-fact contraception. The insertion should be done within seventy-two hours after a pregnancy test comes back negative. An IUD should not be put in if you were already pregnant, but didn't know it, before the condom broke. This could lead to serious problems.

Of course you must be a good low-risk candidate for an IUD in the first place even to consider this option. For exam-

you should be in a stable monogamous relationship in order to reduce the risk of contracting a sexually transmitted disease, and ideally have had at least one child. You should also, of course, plan to continue using the IUD as your birth control method. This form of emergency contraception is not used often in this country, at least in part because so few American women choose IUDs. If you want to find out more about morning-after IUD insertions, talk to your doctor or a health professional at a family planning clinic.

ABORTION

Done early in pregnancy, by an experienced practitioner, in a reputable facility, abortion is very safe and very effective. Under these circumstances, studies have shown, it will also have virtually no effect on a woman's future fertility.

The optimal time to end an unintended pregnancy is probably between about four and eight weeks, or approximately two to six weeks after a missed period. If your menstrual cycle is regular, you would be about two weeks pregnant by the time you miss your first period.

The technique most often used for abortions during this period of time is called suction curettage or vacuum aspiration. This involves passing a narrow, flexible tube through the cervix and into the uterus. A suction device attached to the end of the tube can then extract the tissue that lines the walls of the uterus, where the early pregnancy is implanted. The actual procedure only takes about ten minutes in a doctor's office or clinic. A local anesthetic, and sometimes Valium or another tranquilizer, may be used. After the procedure you will rest, probably for a few hours, until any anesthetic wears off and you feel well enough to go home.

The tissue that is removed from the uterus should be examined to be sure the abortion is complete. Suction curettage very effective, with studies showing success rates approachin̦ 100 percent.

Cramping and bleeding are common after an abortion. Cramps should subside within a day or two; bleeding should slow to spotting within a few days. Serious problems after an abortion are not common, but you should know what symptoms to be alert for, just in case. Be sure to let your doctor know if you have a fever, chills, heavy bleeding containing large clots, fainting, severe abdominal or shoulder pain, or if bleeding persists for more than a week. These could be a sign of infection or another potentially serious problem, such as a ruptured fallopian tube from an undiagnosed ectopic pregnancy, or a perforated uterus.

Very early in pregnancy—at about three to four weeks, or just a week or two after a missed period—a technique called menstrual extraction is sometimes used to remove the uterine lining and end a pregnancy. However, this method has a significantly higher failure rate because the egg is so microscopically small at this stage that it can be missed.

At the other end of the spectrum are abortions done much later in pregnancy, between about sixteen and twenty weeks. (How late abortions are legal depends on the state you live in.) At this stage the abortion may have to be done differently, since the fetus may be too large to be safely or easily removed through the cervix. Sometimes midtrimester abortions are done by injecting salt water (or in some cases, other drugs) through the belly into the uterus and/or by inserting a suppository of a medicine called prostaglandin into the vagina—either of which usually trigger laborlike contractions that expel the fetus.

Another approach is to have a doctor physically open the cervix using special instruments and then, using ultrasound as a guide, remove the fetus through the vagina. This is not a simple

done under general anesthesia and by a
who is familiar with the techniques involved.
ortion is an easy experience, late abortions are
se. Not only is the procedure more of an ordeal,
s also significantly more risky. Prostaglandins can
nausea, vomiting, diarrhea, and intestinal cramps. If salt
ter is accidentally injected into a blood vessel instead of the
uterus, it can lead to shock and death. Too-strong contractions can sometimes cause the uterus to rupture, risking serious bleeding. Removing the fetus through the vagina can
puncture or tear the uterus or cervix and cause heavy bleeding. And general anesthesia poses additional risks.

The bottom line: If an abortion is the right decision for
you, have it done early enough that the safer, simpler suction
curettage can be used.

Finally, just for the record: There is no way that a woman
can safely bring on an abortion herself. Many have tried, in
sometimes unbelievable ways in their desperation. More often
than not, such attempts cause serious health problems—
bleeding, infection, shock—and, in spite of all that, may not
bring an end to the unwanted pregnancy. Death is another
possible outcome of self-induced abortion.

CHEMICAL ABORTION

Ending an unwanted pregnancy with drugs instead of surgery
is something that is done only on an experimental basis in this
country at the moment. *There are no drugs currently approved by the FDA for this use in the United States.*

RU486, OR THE FRENCH ABORTION PILL. This much-
publicized drug is probably the best-known example of a
chemical that can be used to end a pregnancy. Its proper name

is mifepristone. It was developed in France, by a company called Roussel-Uclaf, and is approved for the early termination of pregnancy in England and France. After all the furor arose over its use, the company donated the rights to the drug, including the patent, to the Population Council, a not-for-profit organization devoted to the development of contraceptives.

Although this abortion method has sometimes been written about as if you simply pop a few pills and an unwanted pregnancy is ended, the reality is hardly that simple—or quick. For one thing a woman must first take the pills, then, several days later, return to the clinic to have a prostaglandin (a drug that induces contractions) inserted into her vagina. Within hours, while she remains at the clinic, cramping and bleeding should begin and the contents of the uterus should be expelled. If this doesn't happen, she may need another dose of prostaglandin to bring the abortion about. In the studies available so far (mostly done in Europe, not in the United States), mifepristone appears to be quite effective at bringing about the end of an unwanted pregnancy.

At this point in time mifepristone is essentially unavailable in this country. It is being studied on a very limited research basis at selected family planning clinics. (Exactly which those are is not being publicized because of the possibility of violence against clinic workers and patients by extremist opponents of abortion.) There is some speculation that RU486 might prove to be useful in treating other types of medical conditions. Some examples that have been suggested include using it to induce labor, to treat breast cancer or fibroid tumors of the uterus or Cushing's disease (an abnormality of the adrenal glands), and even, in low doses, for use as a contraceptive. At this point each of these possibilities would require a great deal of study.

Before mifepristone could become widely available for any

use, it would have to go through the same clearly defined approval process required by the FDA as any other new drug. There are some experts in the field who believe that this may never happen because of the political climate in this country.

What might be available some day for nonsurgical abortions is a combination of two drugs that are currently FDA approved, although not for this use. The first is a drug called misoprostol, a prostaglandin prescribed to prevent stomach bleeding. (This drug has also been used in combination with RU486.) The other is methotrexate, a drug used for cancer chemotherapy and as a treatment for tubal pregnancies. Misoprostol and methotrexate are being studied for their use together as a means of inducing an abortion in women who are less than eight weeks pregnant (six weeks from their last period).

In one recent study, reported in the *New England Journal of Medicine*, 178 women who were 63 days pregnant (or less) were first given a shot of methotrexate, then, 5 to 7 days later, they were given a prostaglandin vaginally. (In at least one other study some women were given the prostaglandin by mouth, although this may be less effective.) This usually prompted uterine contractions and a complete abortion within a week. The women who did not have contractions within a week (which happened in 14 percent of them) could choose to have either another dose of vaginal prostaglandin or a suction curettage (vacuum aspiration). Ultimately, well over 90 percent of the women in this study had a successful chemical abortion; no serious side effects or complications occurred. This particular study showed that this technique was safe and effective in a small number of carefully selected women. Research is currently ongoing in this area, and much more information needs to be gathered before the technique is widely used.

As is true with the "morning-after" use of birth control pills, methotrexate and misoprostol are FDA-approved drugs, so their use for chemical abortion is technically legal. However, this regimen should not be administered by someone, even a doctor, who is not familiar with exactly how the drugs should be given and how to handle the possible complications. The FDA has even issued an official reminder in its bulletin that this use of the drugs is investigational. Doctors who are using them in studies go through an official process, which includes approval by an institutional review board at their medical centers, to be sure that matters such as study design and patient informed consent are handled properly.

Cramping, bleeding, and the passage of tissue are expected effects of chemically induced abortion—by either RU486 or methotrexate/misoprostol. Some women have also reported nausea and diarrhea. Sometimes the drugs will not cause a complete abortion, and a woman will later need suction curettage or a D & C (dilation of the cervix and curettage, or scraping, of the uterine lining). Occasionally, heavy bleeding could necessitate a transfusion.

CONTINUING THE PREGNANCY

Studies have shown that women who get pregnant accidentally when they've been using some form of contraception are just as likely to continue the pregnancy as are women who were not using birth control when they got pregnant. When it happens, a woman may decide that her pregnancy is wanted, even if it did happen unexpectedly. If the pregnancy is unwanted, some women will decide to carry the baby to term and then give it up for adoption.

If you decide to let an accidental pregnancy continue, you should of course stop using birth control. An IUD or Norplant implants must be taken out as soon as possible; pills and spermicide use should be discontinued immediately. If you need

STD protection, a condom—either male or female—is safe to use during pregnancy. It is important to see an obstetrician and begin a regimen of good prenatal care.

Common as contraceptive failure is, trying to decide what to do in the case of an unexpected pregnancy is almost always very hard. No matter how sure you are that the choice you make is the right one, it is quite possible that at some point in the future you may find yourself thinking, "If only. . . ." That is natural and normal. You may have fewer haunting thoughts if you feel sure that you considered every possible course of action at the time. Many women have been adamantly opposed to abortion—until they accidentally got pregnant at a time when having a baby was simply not a viable alternative. Similarly women who believe strongly in reproductive freedom and the right to abortion may find themselves unable to end an accidental pregnancy, no matter how inconvenient or distressing it may be. Every woman is different. And the same woman might come to an entirely different decision at a different time, and a different place, in her life.

If you find yourself unexpectedly pregnant, it is important to consider the possibility of carrying the pregnancy to term—just as you would consider each of the other possible courses of action. It is only by thinking through every option and its possible repercussions that you can make a truly informed decision, one that you will be able to live with, with as few regrets as possible, for a lifetime.

Part Eight

FUTURE
CONTRACEPTIVES

CHAPTER

18

_____

WHAT'S ON THE BIRTH CONTROL HORIZON?

Considering how many women use birth control in this country (about 34 million), and considering how long a period of their lives they could potentially need contraception for (thirty-plus years, depending on a woman's personal circumstances), you might think that contraceptives would be the focus of widespread and intensive research efforts.

Well, yes and no.

Although there is some contraceptive research going on right now, there's not as much as you might think, for a number of reasons—which will be discussed shortly. Also the contraceptives now in the works aren't, for the most part, thrilling breakthroughs. Instead they're more on the order of modest improvements and subtle variations on the kinds of birth control we already have to choose from. That's not to say that one of those improvements might not make a method a better choice for you. It certainly might. Just don't expect the "news" in contraceptive research to knock your socks off.

The Stumbling Blocks to Birth Control Research

Contraceptive research is extremely difficult, exceptionally expensive, exceedingly time-consuming, and loaded with potential pitfalls. In fact it has to be one of the single most problematic areas of scientific investigation, for a number of reasons.

AIMING FOR PERFECTION IN EFFECTIVENESS

When it comes to birth control, researchers have to shoot for methods that approach 100 percent effectiveness, since there are contraceptives available right now that come close to this ideal. By comparison, drugs such as ibuprofen (Motrin, Advil, etc.) might offer complete relief from menstrual cramps 70 to 80 percent of the time. Antifungal medications probably cure only about 70 percent of vaginal yeast infections. About 20 percent of the time multiple antibiotics must be prescribed to cure an infection.

SUPER-HIGH SAFETY STANDARDS

Contraceptives also have to be extremely safe. Since birth control is used for long periods of time by healthy young women in the prime of their lives, there is almost zero tolerance for serious side effects. Even more problematic is that if a method fails, a fetus may then be inadvertently exposed to the various chemicals and hormones used in contraceptives.

In contrast, many people are willing to suffer through the sometimes horrifying effects of chemotherapy, just to take an extreme example, because those drugs can be literally life-saving. The same holds true to a lesser extent for many common treatments, such as high blood pressure medication, which can cause impotence in men, and antibiotics, which cause frequent intestinal upsets and occasional serious allergic reactions. Most people simply don't think of birth control in the same way—as beneficial drugs and devices that have certain acceptable trade-offs or risks—probably because birth control doesn't cure anything, or treat anything, or (directly at least) lengthen their lives.

Yet contraceptives do allow you (to a greater or lesser extent, depending on the methods you choose and how carefully you use them) to control the course of your life in what could be argued to be more pivotal ways than almost any other drug or medical device you could name. How many children do you want to have? When would it be best to have them? Women's lives today are profoundly different from those in generations past, at least in part because birth control allows them to choose the answers to these questions.

Birth control also plays a significant role in making the lives of women today both longer and safer. Not all that many years ago childbirth was one of the most common reasons women died in the prime of their lives. It is still a major cause of death in developing countries. And while it's true that tremendous strides have been made in making pregnancy and delivery vastly safer today, it is also undeniable that women who have access to good methods of birth control—and therefore have fewer pregnancies, not to mention desired, planned pregnancies—are most likely to live long and healthy lives. Today the risk of dying during childbirth in the United States is quite small (on the order of 10 per 100,000). Still, the risk of dying while using what most people tend to think of as "risky" birth control methods is dramatically less. For example, the risk of death in nonsmoking Pill users in their twenties and thirties is about ten times lower (around 1 in 100,000) than that of giving birth to a baby.

Still, people do have to realize that nothing in life is entirely without risks—from driving a car to crossing the street to walking down a flight of steps. With birth control and other drugs we do have a right to know what the risks are, but we also need to accept some responsibility for agreeing to assume those risks. Even a one-in-a-million risk is real: Somebody somewhere is going to be the unlucky one.

The Threat of Lawsuits

Another deterrent to contraceptive research is the very real threat of litigation. When birth control methods don't live up to our expectations, we may turn to the legal system to right what we see as wrong. In the past, oral contraceptives and IUDs have been the targets of dozens of lawsuits. Right now Norplant is under the gun. That's not to say that birth control shouldn't be held to the highest standards of safety and effectiveness, because it should. And it's certainly not to say that women who are harmed by any product or device (not only contraceptives) should not have legal recourse, because of course they should. But, realistically, potential legal costs do make companies think twice—or three times or four—about the risks of getting involved in birth control research.

The Current Social and Political Climate

The conservative political climate that is currently making headlines in this country is also not conducive to contraceptive research. Abortion has for a number of years now been a political hot potato, one that shows no signs of cooling off any time soon. If anything, at least some of those who oppose abortion in this country seem to be getting more militant and more extremist in their activities.

Inevitably the furor over abortion spills over onto birth control. For example, it can affect access to contraception for women who use family planning clinics that provide general gynecologic care as well as abortions. It can also make research dollars harder to come by and, once again, make the companies that manufacture and distribute birth control products wary of getting embroiled in the fray. It also makes research on new contraceptives more difficult, since under current laws federal grant money cannot be used for abortion. If a new method being studied doesn't work as well as expected, volunteers may be left on their own to deal with an unexpected pregnancy.

The situation becomes particularly problematic when the line between birth control and abortion seems to blur—take the furor over RU486 (sometimes called the French abortion pill, and now properly named mifepristone) as the most striking recent example. Although this drug is discussed in more detail in chapter 17, suffice it to say here that many contraceptive experts in this country would not be at all surprised if this drug never makes it onto the U.S. market—in large part due to politics.

THE ROLE OF GOVERNMENT TOUGH REGULATORY STANDARDS, TIGHT RESEARCH MONEY

Our government—via agencies such as the Food and Drug Administration (FDA) and the National Institutes of Health (NIH)—has the near-impossible task of trying to maintain a balance between protecting consumers from poorly tested or unsafe drugs and encouraging research and approving new cures as quickly as possible. Sometimes the scales tip one way, sometimes the other. No matter which way the emphasis shifts, somebody's going to scream. It may not be logical, certainly, but it's absolutely understandable: We want both. We want that new treatment for AIDS or breast cancer approved *right now*. Why is the government dragging its heels? But what if, two or ten or twenty years after a supposed "miracle cure" is approved, terrible unanticipated side effects start showing up? Researchers should have known, we think. How could this drug have been approved in the first place?

In terms of birth control research what all of the above currently boils down to is this: ten to twenty years. It can easily take a pharmaceutical company that long, and cost tens of millions of dollars, to boot, to bring a new contraceptive to the market. There are years of preclinical studies to get through, then another five to ten years for the three phases of clinical trials. Once that's done, it can take the FDA two years or more to review the mountain of data that has been collected.

When it comes to government support of basic contraceptive research, such as NIH grant money given to companies and universities, there are only so many dollars to go around. Heart disease, AIDS, and cancer are all top contenders for grants. Rarely is contraception anywhere near the top of the list.

So What Is on the Birth Control Horizon?

Years ago most contraceptive research in this country was carried out by a number of large, diversified pharmaceutical companies, such as Ortho, Searle, Wyeth-Ayerst, and so on. These companies developed, manufactured, and marketed not only birth control but a wide variety of other drugs and medical devices as well. Today some of these familiar pharmaceutical giants still manufacture and market already approved contraceptives, such as condoms, birth control pills, diaphragms, and spermicides, but many are largely out of the picture when it comes to ongoing research.

Today, at least in part because of the obstacles to research mentioned above, much of current research in this country is being done at small independent companies; foreign corporations, such as Organon; and nonprofit organizations, such as the Population Council.

Most of the contraceptives being studied right now are not dramatically different new methods, but rather attempts to improve the methods that are currently available. Many don't require couples to physically do something when they want to have sex, since a large proportion of unexpected pregnancies occur when methods are misused, or not used at all in the heat of the moment. A particular focus is on long-acting methods that protect against pregnancy continuously. Another area of interest, which has grown since the AIDS epidemic, is the development of new and better barrier methods that provide protection against both pregnancy and sexually transmitted diseases.

Let's take a look at each category of birth control (barrier methods, hormonal methods, IUDs, etc.) in turn. Some methods that are close to being approved and marketed will be discussed in fairly specific detail, since they've been widely written up in the scientific literature and tested on hundreds, if not thousands, of volunteers—healthy young women, and in some cases, men. Other areas of birth control research will be discussed in fairly general terms, because, particularly in the early stages, the specifics of product development are considered carefully guarded secrets.

THE NEWS ABOUT BARRIER METHODS

As you may know, the Today contraceptive sponge was taken off the U.S. market in 1995 because of problems meeting current manufacturing standards. At the moment there are

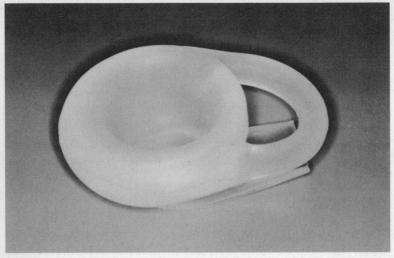

(YAMA, Inc.)

LEA'S SHIELD

apparently no plans for that specific device to be reintro-duced. However, there are several other sponges now in de-velopment, using different types of spermicides (in some cases combinations of more than one spermicide) as well as at least one containing infection-fighting antimicrobial ingredients.

Using birth control to fight off infections, including HIV, as well as preventing pregnancy is in fact one area of great in-terest in the barrier-contraceptive field. Nonoxynol-9, the ac-tive ingredient in spermicides, has also been shown in lab tests to be lethal to many of the germs that cause STDs; research is ongoing into other germ-killing chemicals.

There are at least two new diaphragms being studied at this time. Both are disposable—you would use them once and then throw them away—and both already contain spermicide, so you wouldn't have the extra step of applying it separately. It is hoped that these diaphragms might be able to be left in place for as long as twenty-four hours and remain effective no matter how many times you had sex during that time.

Another new device, called Lea's Shield, is a one-size-fits-all cap that fits over the cervix, with a one-way drain to allow cervical secretions to escape. Lea's Shield is already available, over the counter, in several European countries. A new cervical cap, called FemCap is also in development.

Research on these devices is in various stages, but it's all relatively preliminary. For that reason it is difficult to guess when, if ever, any of them might complete the long and demanding FDA-approval process and become widely available.

The News About IUDs

There is a new type of IUD, known as the Levonorgestrel-T or LNG-20, that has been undergoing studies in Europe, although not, as this book went to press, in the United States. This IUD seems to have some of the best qualities of each of the two IUDs currently available in this country (ParaGard and Progestasert).

Like the Progestasert, the new IUD slowly releases a hormone—in this case it's the progestin levonorgestrel instead of progesterone. One of the major limitations of the Progestasert is that it must be replaced every year, which is significant because the risk of infection is highest shortly after insertion. This new IUD, on the other hand, can be left in place in a woman's uterus for up to five years—a considerable improvement.

Studies done so far suggest that the new IUD is also extremely effective at preventing pregnancy, approximately equal in effectiveness with the ParaGard, which is the IUD most women in this country use. It also appears to be less likely to increase menstrual bleeding than the ParaGard. Although it seems to increase acne in some women, it may also decrease the risk of pelvic infections.

There are at least two other IUDs that are currently available in other countries but are not approved in the United States—such as the Multiload Cu375® and the Novagard®, both copper-containing devices. It seems unlikely, given the small market for IUDs in this country, that either of them will become available in the United States.

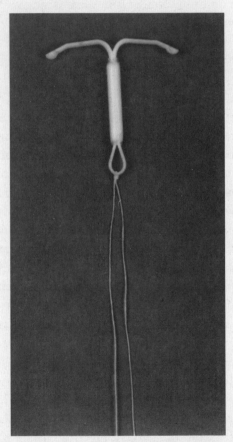

(The Population Council)

LEVONORGESTREL-T IUD

A new type of IUD that had a completely flexible body and was attached to the wall of the uterus was being studied a few years ago in this country. However, since it turned out to be fairly hard for doctors to learn to insert this device, and because early study data showed no huge improvement in safety or side effects over the currently approved ParaGard, studies are currently (and possibly permanently) on hold. This is just one example, among dozens we could name, of what looked to be a promising area of contraceptive research proving to be a probable dead end.

THE NEWS ABOUT ORAL CONTRACEPTIVES

At the moment scientists are tackling two main areas of birth control pill research.

One ongoing goal is to find new progestins that behave in the body as much like a woman's natural progesterone as possible while causing as few negative effects as possible. Specifically the new progestins aim to be very potent (so that they can be effective in small doses) and also very precise in their action. They are very good at their birth control job, while having fewer of the so-called androgenic effects of some progestins, such as acne, the growth of unwanted body hair, and unhealthy changes in lipid (fatty substances) levels in the blood. Two of these new-generation progestins are already on the market in this country (desogestrel and norgestimate) in combination oral contraceptives.

On an entirely different tack, researchers are also working on new biphasic and triphasic pills, tinkering with new variations on how much hormone is in the pills at different times during the month and also with the number of active hormone pills that are to be taken during the cycle. The goal is to find even more precise ways to deliver the minimum possible dose of hormone exactly when it's needed during the cycle to prevent pregnancy.

THE NEWS ABOUT IMPLANTS

By the time this book is published, a two-rod implant from the makers of Norplant (Wyeth-Ayerst) may already be available. The FDA New Drug Application (NDA) was filed in 1995, and approval might be expected sometime in 1997. (It's already approved in Finland and China.) The significant improvement here is that this version of Norplant has just two matchstick-sized hormone-containing rods, as opposed to the original's six. This makes insertion and removal significantly easier. The trade-off is that the two-rod system will last for three years instead of five. It is possible that this length of time will be extended as clinical trials on the new implant continue.

Also in the works is a new implant that goes by the name Implanon. This version has just one rod containing a different type of progestin (3-keto-desogestrel). It is designed with a special insertion device that should make it much easier to correctly place the rod under the skin. Implanon is expected to be effective for three years. The first two years of study in the U.S. have just been completed, and the new device could be available in as little as three years.

There are at least two more single-rod implant systems also in the early stages of development at this time.

Preliminary research is also under way on biodegradable implants, ones that would simply dissolve over time and not have to be removed. One of the stumbling blocks with research on degradable implants is that they might be very difficult to take out after a certain point if a woman wished to become pregnant or change birth control methods.

The News About Sterilization

There is a new type of clasp for closing off the fallopian tubes, called a Filshie clip. It is now available in Europe, and could be approved for use in the United States in as little as a year or so. The device is designed to do as little damage as possible to the tube, thus, it is hoped, increasing the odds that sterilizations might be more often successfully reversed.

Researchers have also been experimenting with various chemicals that could be injected into the tubes to seal them closed. None of these look like they will be widely available anytime soon.

New Approaches

VAGINAL RINGS. Hormone-impregnated vaginal rings of one sort or another have been the subject of contraceptive research for decades. Imagine a donut-shaped ring slightly smaller than a diaphragm but without the diaphragm's soft

(The Population Council)

NESTORONE PROGESTIN VAGINAL RING

latex dome, and that's essentially what a vaginal ring would look like. The possible advantages of this approach to birth control would be to have a method that would be highly effective (as are other hormone-based methods, such as the Pill or Norplant) and easily reversible, since a woman could put it in and take it out herself. Hormones delivered in this way might also have fewer systemic effects and therefore possibly have a lower incidence of the side effects that occur with hormonal methods.

Some of the problems that are still being ironed out in vaginal-ring research include finding exactly the right material from which to make the ring itself, figuring out ways to have the hormone be released slowly and evenly over time, and zeroing in on an optimal size for the ring, so that it's big enough to stay correctly in place over much longer periods of time than the diaphragm but not so big that it becomes irritating to the tissues of the vagina or uncomfortable to wear.

One ring that's currently being studied contains progestin only, so it's somewhat similar to Norplant or Depo-Provera shots, except that it would be instantly reversible. Studies have shown that it tends to cause irregular bleeding patterns like those of the other progestin-only contraceptives.

Another ring under investigation contains a combination of estrogen and progestin, like the Pill, that would be inserted and worn continuously for three weeks, then taken out for one, during which a woman would have her period, just as she would if she were on oral contraceptives.

If the rings are uncomfortable during sex, they can be taken out for a few hours without making them less effective; however, every time a woman takes the ring out, she runs the risk of forgetting to put it back in.

At this point in time it is difficult to hazard a guess about when vaginal rings might become available.

BIRTH CONTROL "PATCHES." Another possibility that's even farther down the road from general availability is contraceptive skin patches, similar to the estrogen patches now available for hormone replacement therapy in post-menopausal women. The advantages of this approach for contraception could be high effectiveness combined with immediate reversibility and ease of use—since you would be protected from pregnancy as long as your patch was on. You'd just have to remember to exchange it for a new one after the appropriate interval. Although this is an approach that may well be available at some point in the future, at the moment there are a number of problems that researchers have yet to resolve. (For example, progestins are not as readily absorbed through the skin as estrogen is.)

There is a great deal of theoretical interest in the development of some type of "contraceptive vaccine"—an injection of a chemical or drug that would work to prevent pregnancy in one of a number of different ways. But at the moment this particular avenue of research would appear to be, at best, years from fruition.

THE NEWS ABOUT MALE CONTRACEPTIVES

In many ways male contraceptives are even more of a challenge to develop than are those for women. For one thing a male birth control method must stop the constant production of millions of sperm. Compared to that, female contraception, which "merely" has to stop the release of one little egg each month sounds like a simple task.

One problem researchers have discovered is that drugs that effectively suppress sperm production also tend to damage the testes, so that fertility might end up permanently impaired. Irreversible infertility turned out to be one of the problems with gossypol, the controversial male contraceptive studied most widely in China that made headlines several years ago. The World Health Organization (WHO) stopped supporting gossypol research in 1990 because of concerns about its effectiveness and toxicity.

Arguably the most promising approach at the moment—although there are still a number of bugs to be worked out—has been using testosterone injections for male contraception. Testosterone shots work by suppressing the production of the brain hormones that prompt sperm production. Researchers are looking at different schedules for the shots (weekly, monthly, every three months), and the possibility of combining testosterone with other drugs for better effectiveness with fewer side effects. Most experts would probably agree that wide availability of this method is years away.

Researchers are also exploring a variety of ways (creams, patches, even implants) to deliver various sperm-suppressing or sperm-damaging drugs, but these, too, are all at best many years down the road.

Also years from general availability is the possibility of reversible vasectomy using removable plugs in the vas, as well as permanent, no-surgery sterilization via injections of various chemicals into the vas.

Researchers are looking into new latex-free condom materials, and also different designs—including, for example, a "baggy bottom" condom, aimed at increasing sensation.

There, in a nutshell, are some of the highlights of current contraceptive research. Some of these methods, even those that seem the most promising today, may hit an unforeseen stumbling block tomorrow and drop out of the race. Other innovations will come along and take their place. But even if all the best and brightest of tomorrow's possibilities were to fly through the research-and-approval processes with nary a snag, one thing remains clear: There is, as we have maintained all along, no perfect contraceptive—not even on the drawing boards.

Each of the birth control methods available today, and each of those in the various stages of research and development, has its strengths and its weaknesses. Each will work better for some women than it will for others. And, equally important, the contraceptive that is the ideal choice for you right now will probably *not* be the best possible option a few years down the road. Five years from now one of the new methods discussed in this chapter might become available, and might be just the right choice for you at that point in your life.

No contraceptive is perfect, but at the same time many of the birth control options out there right now are really very good. Today we can choose from contraceptives that are extremely safe, highly effective, widely available, easily reversible, often quite easy to use, and very diverse. Whether you are choosing a method for the first time, or the second, or the third, the principle remains the same: The more you know about birth control—the more you read, the more information you give to and elicit from your doctor, the more you quiz your friends for the nitty-gritty details—the more power you will have to zero in on the method that will work best for your health and your life, right now and in the future.

Glossary

abdomen/abdominal: the belly; the lower half of the interior of the human body, containing the intestines, liver, gallbladder, spleen, and, in females, the reproductive organs.

AIDS, or acquired immunodeficiency syndrome: an incurable illness caused by the HIV virus, which attacks the immune system and leaves the body vulnerable to many serious infections.

amenorrhea: the absence of menstrual bleeding—"skipped" periods.

anemia: a decrease of oxygen-carrying red blood cells or hemoglobin in the blood.

anesthesia: medications that block pain during surgery. With **general anesthesia** the patient is asleep and the entire body is pain-free. With **regional anesthesia**, feeling is deadened in a portion of the body, such as a limb or the lower half of the body (a "spinal"). **Local anesthesia** numbs only the immediate area.

anus: the opening at the lower end of the intestinal tract from which bowel movements emerge, located to the rear of the external sex organs.

barrier contraceptive: a method of birth control that works by physically or chemically blocking sperm from reaching an egg.

basal temperature: your body temperature when you first wake up in the morning, before even getting out of bed.

benign: noncancerous.

Billings method: a technique of predicting ovulation by noting regular monthly changes in cervical mucus, often used as a method of natural family planning.

bladder: an organ in the lower abdomen that collects and stores urine.

breakthrough bleeding: vaginal bleeding that occurs between menstrual periods.

cervical cancer: cancer of the cervix or mouth of the uterus.

cervical cap: a barrier contraceptive device designed to fit snugly over the cervix.

cervical mucus: fluid produced by the cervix that undergoes predictable changes during the menstrual cycle.

cervix: the narrow lower end of the uterus that protrudes into the top of the vagina.

chlamydia: a common sexually transmitted infection that can cause pelvic inflammatory disease and sterility in women.

cholesterol: a substance found in food and produced by the body that in excess amounts can cause narrowing, even complete blockage, of blood vessels, resulting in heart attack and stroke.

circumcised: when the penis has had a fold of skin at the tip, called the foreskin, surgically removed.

clinical trial: the testing of a new drug or device on human volunteers before it is approved by the FDA for general use.

combination oral contraceptives: birth control pills containing both estrogen and progestin.

conception: the implantation of a fertilized egg into the uterine lining.

condom (male): a barrier contraceptive put over the penis to protect against pregnancy and/or sexually transmitted diseases.

condom (female): a barrier contraceptive inserted so that it lines a woman's vagina to protect against pregnancy and/or sexually transmitted diseases.

contraception: any of a number of techniques used for the prevention of pregnancy.

contraindication: a condition or circumstance that makes the use of a drug or device unsafe (an "absolute contraindication") or less safe (a "relative contraindication").

corpus luteum: a hormone-producing area on the ovary that forms after an egg is released.

cyst: a self-contained fluid-filled sac that forms in the body.

cystitis: a bladder infection.

Depo-Provera: a long-acting contraceptive injection.

diaphragm: a barrier contraceptive device that is inserted into the vagina so that it covers the cervix.

douche: a rinsing out of the vagina.

ectopic pregnancy: a pregnancy that occurs outside of the uterus, most often in the fallopian tubes.

effectiveness: how well a particular birth control method prevents pregnancy. **Theoretical effectiveness** is the lowest possible pregnancy rate that would be expected if the method was used perfectly every time. **Typical effectiveness** is a higher pregnancy rate that includes the misuses and errors that commonly occur.

ejaculation: the release of semen and sperm from the penis during orgasm.

electrocautery: an electric knife that can be used to cut and/or fuse tissue; specifically the device used to seal the fallopian tubes during tubal ligation.

embolism: a clot or air bubble that travels in the blood, which can lodge in a blood vessel, blocking the blood flow to a vital organ.

endometrial cancer: cancer of the lining of the uterus.

endometrium: the lining of the uterus.

epilepsy: a disease characterized by seizures.

estrogen: one of the two main hormones produced naturally by the body that regulate the female reproductive system (the other is progesterone).

failure rate: the frequency with which pregnancy occurs while using a particular contraceptive.

fallopian tubes: the narrow passageways through which the egg travels, connecting the ovaries to the uterus.

Food and Drug Administration (FDA): the U.S. government agency charged with ensuring that drugs and medical devices are both safe and effective before they can be sold to the public.

female condom: see condom (female)

fertility: the female's ability to become pregnant, and the male's ability to cause a pregnancy.

fertility awareness: various techniques that allow a woman to determine the times in her menstrual cycle when she is more and less likely to get pregnant.

fertilization: the process of the male's sperm penetrating the female's egg (ovum).

fibroid tumors: benign growths in the wall of the uterus.

fimbria: the fingerlike projections on the ends of the fallopian tubes nearest to the ovaries.

follicle: a blisterlike sac on the surface of an ovary that contains an egg.

genital: relating to the reproductive organs.

genital warts: growths caused by some strains of the human papillomavirus (HPV), which can appear on the skin of the external genitals or inside a woman's vagina and on her cervix.

gonorrhea: a common sexually transmitted infection that can cause pelvic inflammatory disease and sterility in women.

gynecologist: a physician who specializes in the care of the female reproductive system.

herpes: a common sexually transmitted infection caused by the herpes simplex virus.

HIV, or human immunodeficiency virus: the incurable virus that causes AIDS.

hormones: chemicals produced by the body that control various body functions.

human papillomavirus (HPV): a virus that comes in dozens of variations, or "strains." Some strains have been linked to genital warts; some (although not necessarily the same ones) have been linked to cervical cancer; others appear to be completely benign.

hymen: tissue circling the opening to the vagina, which may naturally be somewhat thick and tough, or thin and nearly invisible. Because of these natural variations, looking at the hymen does not reveal whether or not a woman is a virgin.

hysterectomy: surgery to remove the uterus, and sometimes the fallopian tubes and ovaries as well.

implantation: the embedding of a fertilized egg into the uterine lining.

infertility: the inability to get pregnant, or, for a man, cause a pregnancy in a woman.

intrauterine device (IUD): a small device inserted into the uterus to prevent pregnancy.

jaundice: a yellowing of the skin and whites of the eyes that is a symptom of liver problems.

labia: the lips of the external genital area of a woman.

labia majora: the larger, outer, hair-covered lips.

labia minora: the smaller inner lips covering the vaginal opening.

laparoscope: a long, narrow tube used to view and operate inside the abdomen.

latex: a naturally occurring rubber that most condoms, diaphragms, and cervical caps are made of.

lesions: areas of abnormal tissue, sores, growths.

melasma: a darkening of the skin, particularly of the face, that can occur with oral contraceptive use and during pregnancy.

menopause: the ending of menstrual cycles, and fertility, in women.

menstrual cycle: the month-long cycle of the reproductive organs, which includes regular changes in hormone levels, the release of an egg from the ovaries, and the preparation of the lining of the uterus for pregnancy—followed by the shedding of the uterine lining during menstruation if pregnancy does not occur.

menstruation: regular, cyclic bleeding from the uterus that occurs approximately once a month during a woman's fertile years, except during pregnancy.

migraine: a particular type of headache, often severe.

minilaparotomy: surgical sterilization of a woman through an incision in the lower abdomen.

minipills: oral contraceptives that contain a progestin only, no estrogen.

monogamy: exclusive sex. **Mutual monogamy** refers to partners in a couple who have sex only with each other. **Serial monogamy** refers to people who have sex with only one partner for a period of time.

natural birth control: the avoidance of unwanted pregnancy without the use of drugs or devices, achieved by observing the natural changes in a woman's body during the menstrual cycle that indicate when conception is more and less likely.

nonoxynol-9: the active, sperm-killing ingredient in most vaginal spermicides.

Norplant: small, long-acting contraceptive rods that are inserted under the skin of a woman's upper inner arm.

obstetrician (obstetrician-gynecologist): a physician who specializes in the care of women during pregnancy and childbirth.

oral contraceptives: birth control pills that contain either estrogen and progestin (combination oral contraceptives) or a progestin alone ("minipills").

oral sex: sexual stimulation of one partner by the other by means of the mouth.

orgasm: the sexual climax.

os: the mouth of the cervix (*os* means "mouth" in Latin).

osteoporosis: a thinning and weakening of the bones.

ovarian cancer: cancer of the ovaries.

ovaries: the two oval organs, one on each side of the uterus, that hold a woman's eggs.

oviducts: another word for fallopian tubes—the passageways through which eggs travel from the ovary to the uterus.

ovulate/ovulation: the release of a mature egg from an ovary.

Pap smear: a test of the cells of the cervix designed to detect noncancerous cervical changes and cervical cancer.

ParaGard: one of two IUDs currently available in the United States.

PID, or pelvic inflammatory disease: an inflammation and infection of the upper organs of reproduction (uterus, ovaries, tubes) that can cause infertility (if it attacks and scars the fallopian tubes).

placebo: an inactive pill, sometimes called a sugar pill.

polycystic ovarian syndrome: a condition in which many fluid-filled blisters form on the ovary, and a cause of infertility.

polyurethane: a type of man-made plastic that the female condom, and at least one brand of male condom, is made of.

progestin: a man-made version of the hormone progesterone, which is one of the two main hormones regulating a woman's menstrual cycle. Progestins are used in many contraceptives, including birth control pills, Norplant implants, and Depo-Provera shots.

Progestasert: one of two IUDs currently available in this country. The Progestasert has progesterone as its active ingredient.

progesterone: one of two naturally occurring hormones that regulate a woman's reproductive system (the other is estrogen).

prolactin: a hormone produced by nursing mothers that stimulates milk production and suppresses ovulation.

Reality female condom: a polyurethane sheath, inserted into the vagina, used to prevent pregnancy and prevent the spread of sexually transmitted diseases.

rhythm: a way of avoiding pregnancy by counting the days of the menstrual cycle to determine times of likely fertility. Sometimes called the calendar method. Rhythm alone is not considered an effective means of birth control.

scrotum: the hair-covered sac of skin that hangs behind the penis in a man and holds the testicles, which manufacture sperm.

semen: the fluid released from the penis during ejaculation.

sperm: the male cell of reproduction that joins with a female's egg to produce a pregnancy.

sperm antibodies: substances that can be found in some men's blood, particularly after a vasectomy, that may interfere with fertility.

spermicides: foams, creams, jellies, and so on, containing the active ingredient nonoxynol-9, that are designed to kill sperm and reduce the chances of conception.

spotting: light bleeding between menstrual periods.

staining: bleeding between menstrual periods that is so light, it only "stains" or colors a woman's cervical mucus or toilet tissue.

STD (sexually transmitted disease): an infection that can be passed from one person to another through sexual contact (vaginal, oral, anal, etc.).

sympto-thermal techniques: a variety of strategies used to determine a woman's fertile and nonfertile days. Most common are the charting of a woman's basal body temperature and observation of the changes in her cervical mucus.

testicles: the organs that manufacture a man's sperm, which are located in the scrotum (the hair-covered sac of skin that hangs behind the penis).

the Pill: oral contraceptives.

thromboembolism: a clot that breaks loose and travels through the blood vessels.

thrombophlebitis: inflammation of, and clot formation in, the veins, usually in the legs.

toxic shock syndrome (TSS): a life-threatening, although relatively uncommon, infection caused by the by-products of certain bacteria that has been linked to tampon use and that some have theorized may be more likely in women who use diaphragms and cervical caps.

trichomoniasis: a common vaginal infection that can be sexually transmitted.

triglycerides: fatty substances in the blood, which in excess can increase the risk of heart attack (particularly in women) and stroke.

tubal ligation: the closing off of the fallopian tubes during female sterilization.

tubal pregnancy: a potentially life-threatening pregnancy that occurs in one of the fallopian tubes instead of in the uterus. Also called ectopic pregnancy.

urethra: the tube through which urine flows from the bladder to exit the body.

urinary tract infection (UTI): an infection of the bladder and urethra.

uterus: the pear-sized muscular organ where a fetus develops. Also called the womb.

vagina: the tube of flexible, stretchable tissue that connects a woman's outer sex organs (labia, clitoris, etc.) to the inner sex organs (uterus, tubes, ovaries).

vaginal spermicides: jellies, foams, and tablets that are put into the vagina to kill sperm.

vas deferens: tiny tubes through which sperm travel from the testicles (where sperm are made) to the penis (where sperm are released during ejaculation).

vasectomy: the severing of the vas deferens, the tiny tubes in the male reproductive system that carry sperm.

virgin: a man or woman who has not had sex.

vulva: the external genital area of a woman.

APPENDIX

WHERE TO GO FOR MORE INFORMATION

Phone Numbers

For more information as well as confidential answers to questions about AIDS prevention and/or condoms, call:
 The National AIDS Hot Line: 800-342-2437 (AIDS),
 24 hours, 7 days a week
 Spanish: 800-344-7432 (SIDA), 7 days, 8 A.M.–2 A.M. EST
 TYY Service for the Deaf: 800-243-7889, M–F, 10 A.M.–
 10 P.M. EST

For confidential information about herpes, call:
 The Herpes Resource Center, to order written material—
 800-230-6039, M–F, 9 A.M.–7 P.M. EST
 National Herpes Hot Line offers phone counseling,
 referrals, medical information—919-361-8488, M–F,
 9 A.M.–7 P.M. EST

For confidential information about all types of sexually transmitted diseases and their prevention and treatment, call:

The National STD Hot Line: 800-227-8922, M–F, 8 A.M.–11 P.M. EST

If you have questions about the following products, each has a toll-free number (other companies may also have 800-numbers—check the box or package insert):

- Advance 1 Easy Step Pregnancy Test: 800-526-3979
- Clearblue Easy Pregnancy Test Kit, or Clearplan Easy One-Step Ovulation Predictor: 800-883-EASY
- e.p.t. pregnancy test: 800-562-0266 or 800-223-0182, M–F; if you speak Spanish, call: 800-3ESPANOL
- Reality Female Condom: 800-274-6601

Organizations

The Alan Guttmacher Institute
120 Wall Street
New York, NY 10005
This nonprofit organization conducts research on family planning issues and publishes a magazine called *Family Planning Perspectives*. Although they don't deal directly with the public, you are likely to see their highly respected experts, and the research they produce, quoted frequently in the media.

The American College of Obstetricians and Gynecologists (ACOG)
409 Twelfth Street, SW
Washington, DC 20024
This organization of board-certified specialists can provide free single copies of educational brochures on many topics, including all types of contraception and sexually transmitted diseases. To request one, send a business-size self-addressed

stamped envelope to the Resource Center at the above address. The ACOG cannot refer patients to individual doctors.

The American Social Health Association (ASHA)
Research Triangle Park, NC 27709
This nonprofit organization is devoted to STD prevention and education. It runs the National STD Hot Line and the National AIDS Hot Line, under contract with the U.S. Centers for Disease Control and Prevention. (Hot-line numbers are listed in the "Phone Numbers" section.) They will also send you free written information on a variety of topics relating to sexually transmitted diseases and sexual health in general if you call the ASHA Healthline: 800-972-8500, 24 hours, 7 days.

AVSC, International
79 Madison Avenue
New York, NY 10016
212-561-8000
AVSC stands for Access to Voluntary and Safe Contraception. This nonprofit organization is best known for its work in the area of voluntary sterilization. They will answer questions from both the lay public and doctors and/or send written material about both male and female sterilization, and about other birth control methods as well. They can also help you find a doctor who does no-scalpel vasectomies.

Cervical Cap Ltd.
430 Monterey Avenue, Suite 1B
Los Gatos, CA 95030
408-395-2100
Cervical caps are available to doctors and family planning clinics, who provide them to women by prescription. The company has two videos available, one for doctors, one how-

to-use-it for their patients. They cost $50 and $30, respectively, or $75 for both.

Family of the Americas Foundation
P.O. Box 1170
Dunkirk, MD 20754
301-627-3346

This nonprofit organization supports teachers of the ovulation method (OM) in more than one hundred countries around the world. For free written information and phone counseling about this method of natural family planning, call 800-443-3395 (M–F 9 A.M.–5 P.M. EST). They also offer an OM "starter kit," which includes a videotape, a book, and charts, for $39.95. (Note: The authors recommend personal instruction before trying to use this or any "natural" method.)

The Norplant Foundation

This nonprofit organization provides Norplant contraceptive implants free to some low-income women who do not qualify for Medicaid. Also, if you already have Norplant implants and wish to have them removed, they can help you find a doctor who will do this for free if you can't afford it otherwise and aren't covered by Medicaid. Their phone number is 800-760-9093 or 703-706-5933. If you speak Spanish, there will be someone available who can help you at the same number.

Planned Parenthood Federation of America, Inc.
810 Seventh Avenue
New York, NY 10019
and
1120 Connecticut Avenue, NW
Washington, DC 20036

There are more than nine hundred Planned Parenthood clinics across the United States. They offer reproductive health care and education in the areas of birth control, abortion, STD diagnosis and treatment, and general reproductive health care (Pap smears, checkups, etc.). Some clinics also offer a full range of prenatal care, obstetrical care, and well-baby services. All clinics are open to women; some also treat men. To be automatically connected to the clinic nearest you, call: 800-230-PLAN (7526).

Books

The Best Intentions: Unintended Pregnancy and the Well-being of Children and Families
Institute of Medicine
Sarah S. Brown and Leon Eisenberg, editors
National Academy Press, Washington, DC, 1995
A timely and thorough government report from a distinguished panel of experts, examining the complex issues involved in why so many unintended pregnancies occur in the United States and including suggestions for what might be done about it.

The Billings Method
Dr. Evelyn Billings and Ann Westmore
Ballantine Books, New York, NY, 1983
A guide to the Billings Ovulation Method (cervical mucus method).

Contraceptive Technology, 16th Revised Edition
Robert A. Hatcher, M.D., M.P.H.; James Trussell, Ph.D.; Felicia Stewart, M.D.; Gary K. Stewart, M.D., M.P.H.; Deborah Kowal, M.A., P.A.; Felicia Guest, M.P.H., C.H.E.S.; Willard Cates, Jr., M.D. M.P.H.; Michael S. Policar, M.D., M.P.H.

Irvington Publishers, Inc., New York, NY, 1994
This textbook for doctors, nurses, and other health professionals interested in family planning has sometimes been called the bible of contraception information. Thorough, fact-filled, opinionated, and often quite technical, it is written by a team of well-known experts.

A Cooperative Method of Natural Birth Control
Margaret Nofziger
The Book Publishing Company
P.O. Box 99
Summertown, TN, 38483
1-800-695-2241
A clear, simple guide to charting temperature, cervical mucus, and other physical symptoms to achieve or avoid pregnancy without drugs or other contraceptive devices.

Developing New Contraceptives: Obstacles and
Opportunities
Institute of Medicine
Luigi Mastroianni, Jr.; Peter J. Donaldson; Thomas T. Kane, editors
National Academy Press, Washington, DC, 1990
A fascinating government report by top authorities in the field on the way contraceptives are developed and approved in this country.

Emergency Contraception: The Nation's Best-Kept Secret
Robert A. Hatcher, M.D.; James Trussell, Ph.D.; Felicia Stewart, M.D.; Susan Howells, M.P.A.; Caroline R. Russell; Deborah Kowal, P.A.
Bridging the Gap Communications, Inc., Atlanta, GA, 1995, 800-721-6990

A tiny paperback, by several of the same authors as *Contraceptive Technology*, describing how the morning-after pill works, how it's used, and where (state by state) you can find a doctor or clinic who knows about this use of oral contraceptive pills.

The Physicians' Desk Reference (or PDR)
Medical Economics Data Production Company, Montvale, NJ, 1995
Updated yearly, this huge reference book includes pictures of and detailed, highly technical information about most (but not all) of the prescription drugs that are currently approved for use in the United States by the Food and Drug Administration (FDA). If you'd like to read through the complete package insert for, say, Norplant or oral contraceptives, this is the book for you.

The Physicians' Desk Reference for Nonprescription Drugs
Medical Economics Data Production Company, Montvale NJ, 1995
A similar, although less inclusive, volume covering over-the-counter medications and devices (including some pregnancy tests and spermicides).

The Pill: A Biography of the Drug That Changed the World
Bernard Asbell
Random House, New York, NY, 1995
A fascinating, readable overview of the development and evolution of oral contraceptives.

INDEX

Abdominal pain, of ectopic
    pregnancy, 35, 140, 152
Abortion
    chemical, 210–13
    late, 209–10
    menstrual extraction, 209
    political climate and, 220–21
    safety and side effects of, 208,
        209, 210
    suction curettage (vacuum
        aspiration), 208–9, 213
Abstinence, periodic, 12, 18, 19
    See also Fertility awareness
        methods
Acne, 140, 153, 164, 225, 227
Age
    contraceptive choice and, 16–17,
        18–19, 41
    irregular bleeding and, 154
Air embolism, 191, 192
Alan Guttmacher Institute, 5, 19, 24,
    203, 248
Amenorrhea, 31, 148, 153, 159
American College of Obstetricians
    and Gynecologists (ACOG),
    5, 248–49
Aminoglutethimide, 163

Anal sex, condom protection in, 66,
    68
Androgenic effects, 131, 140, 227
Anemia, 122, 137, 164
Anesthesia, 185, 190, 195, 208, 210
Antibiotics, 153
Anus, 28

Barrier methods. See Cervical caps;
    Condoms; Condoms,
    female; Diaphragms;
    Spermicides
Basal thermometers, 52, 57
Billings method. See Cervical mucus
    method
Birth control
    barrier methods. See Cervical
        caps; Condoms; Condoms,
        female; Diaphragms;
        Spermicides
    breast feeding as, 35–36
    history of past use, 42
    implant system. See Norplant
    information sources on, 247–52
    natural. See Fertility awareness
        methods
    number of users, 1

perfect *vs* typical use, 13, 14
safety standards for, 218–19
sterilization. *See* Tubal ligation;
    Vasectomy
See also Hormone-based
    methods; Intrauterine
    devices (IUDs)
Birth control decision, 9–26
convenience in, 14–16
cost in, 13–14
doctor consultation on. *See*
    Doctor, talking to
effectiveness in, 11–13
fertility factors in, 17, 20
health factors in, 25, 43–44
partner's attitude in, 23
at stages in life, 16–17, 18–19, 41
STD protection and, 20–22,
    42–43
Birth control failure, 203–4
cervical caps, 12, 105, 107
condoms (female), 12, 75
condoms (male), 12, 66
Depo-Provera, 12, 158
diaphragms, 12, 93
fertility awareness methods, 12,
    56, 57, 59
IUDs, 12, 173
minipill, 136
Norplant, 12, 146
options in, 205–14
perfect and typical use, 12
pill, 12, 121
spermicides, 12, 83–84
tubal ligation, 12, 187
vasectomy, 12, 196
Birth control pill. *See* Pill
Birth control research, 217–33
on barrier methods, 223–25
companies involved in, 222–23
on implants, 228
on IUDs, 225–27
on male contraceptives, 231–33
obstacles to, 218–22
on pill, 227–28
on skin patches, 231
on sterilization, 229
on vaccine, 231
on vaginal rings, 229–30
Birth defects, 125, 140

spermicides and, 86, 97
Bleeding
abnormal, 132, 154, 166
after abortion, 209, 210
amenorrhea, 31, 148, 153, 159
Depo-Provera and, 159, 160, 164
irregular, 123, 131, 137–38, 191
IUDs and, 175
in menstrual cycle, 32
Norplant and, 148–49, 153, 154
progestin-estrogen pills and, 117,
    119, 126, 127
progestin-only pills and, 130, 135,
    137–38
after tubal ligation, 191
after vasectomy, 198
Blood clots, 116
in legs, 43, 132, 152, 162
in veins, 127–28, 139, 152
Body-hair growth, 131, 140, 153,
    227
Breast cancer, 211
Depo-Provera and, 162, 163–64
oral contraceptives and, 43,
    128–29, 132, 142
Breast disease, benign, 122
Breastfeeding
as birth control, 35–36
Depo-Provera in, 160
minipills in, 137, 141
Norplant in, 147
Breast tenderness, 126, 140, 142,
    153, 164

Calendar method. *See* Rhythm
    method
Carbamazepine, 140
Carbon dioxide embolism, 191, 192
Cardiovascular problems, 128, 139,
    152
Cervical cancer, 21, 44, 67, 95
Cervical caps, 30, 42, 101–11,
    249–50
candidates for, 108–9
cost of, 14, 106
design of, 101
effectiveness of, 12, 104–5
inserting, 103, 104
manufacturers of, 101
operation of, 102

Cervical caps *(cont'd)*
  pros and cons of, 15, 16, 106–7
  removing, 103
  research on, 225
  reversibility of, 107
  safety and side effects of, 103,
    107–8
  spermicide with, 102, 103, 105
  tips for using, 110–11
Cervical mucus, 118, 134, 138, 145,
  149, 158, 161
Cervical mucus method, 49, 50–52,
  53, 58, 250
Cervix, 29–30, 42, 172, 209
Chancroid, 24
Chemical abortion, 210–13
Childbearing years, stages of, 16–17
Chlamydia, 24, 58, 67
Cholesterol level, 117, 126, 132, 163
Cilia, 31
Climax, 55
Clitoris, 27–28
Coitus interruptus (withdrawal), 12,
  26, 55
Conception, 32–34, 36–37
Condoms, 31, 43, 44
  age of users, 17, 18, 19
  brand names, 63, 64
  candidates for, 71
  cost of, 13, 14, 67
  effectiveness of, 12, 13, 66–67, 68
  materials used in, 64, 67, 70
  men's attitude toward, 23, 70, 71
  popularity of, 26, 63
  pros and cons of, 15, 67, 70
  putting on, 64–66
  research on, 232
  reversibility of, 71
  safety of, 71
  spermicide with, 67, 68, 69, 84
  STD protection of, 42, 67, 68, 123
  tips for using, 68–69
Condoms, female, 12, 14, 26, 72–80
  candidates for, 78
  cost of, 76
  effectiveness of, 75–76
  insertion of, 73–74
  manufacture of, 72
  pros and cons of, 76–77
  removal of, 75

reversibility of, 77
  safety of, 78
  tips for using, 79
Contraception, 4, 15
Contraceptive Technology, 4–5, 12,
  14, 56, 105
Corpus luteum, 33–34
Cramping, after abortion, 209, 210
Creams, 81, 82
Cushing's disease, 211
Cystitis, 44

D & C (dilation and curettage), 213
Dalkon Shield, 1, 175
Depo-Provera, 9, 42, 43, 156–66
  candidates for, 165–66
  cost of, 14, 158–59
  effectiveness of, 12, 158
  injection of, 157
  operation of, 157–58
  popularity of, 156
  pros and cons of, 15, 16, 159–61
  reversibility of, 161–62
  safety and side effects of, 31,
    162–65
Depression, 131, 132, 164
Desogestrel, 116, 127, 128, 227
Diaphragms, 30, 42, 44, 89–100
  age of users, 18, 19
  candidates for, 100
  cleaning and storing, 91
  cost of, 14, 94–95
  effectiveness of, 12, 93–94
  fitting, 90, 94, 96
  inserting, 91, 92, 96, 98
  manufacturers of, 89
  partner's attitude toward, 23
  popularity of, 26, 89
  pros and cons of, 15, 95–96
  removing, 91, 96, 98
  research on, 224–25
  reversibility of, 97
  safety and side effects of, 97, 99
  spermicide with, 83, 90, 93–94,
    95, 96, 98–99
  tips for using, 98–99
Dilantin, 43
Dizziness, 140, 153, 164
Doctor, talking to, 38–46
  opening up, 39–40

personal history in, 40–44, 45
written information from, 44, 46
Douche, 26, 88
Drug interactions
    with Depo-Provera, 163
    with Norplant, 153
    with oral contraceptives, 127, 140

Ectopic pregnancy, 34–35, 140, 152,
    177–78
Ejaculation, 66
Electrocautery, 185, 190
Embryo, 34
Emergency contraceptive pills, 12
Endometrial cancer, 25, 122, 128,
    131, 154, 164, 166
Endometriosis, 35, 43, 130, 164
Endometrium, 30, 33, 34, 119
Epididymitis, 199
Estrogen, 33, 34, 116
    synthetic. See Pill
Ethinyl estradiol, 116

Fallopian tubes, 30, 31, 33, 34–35,
    183, 209
    See also Ectopic pregnancy; Tubal
    ligation
Family Planning Perspectives, 4
Female condoms. See Condoms,
    female
FemCap, 225
Fertility
    factors determining, 17, 20
    personal history of, 41
Fertility awareness methods, 30, 31,
    40, 49–60, 109
    age of users, 18, 19
    candidates for, 59
    cervical mucus (ovulation), 12, 49,
        53, 58
    cost of, 57
    counseling in, 60
    with diaphragm, 93
    effectiveness of, 12, 36–37,
        56–57, 59
    pros and cons of, 57–58
    reversibility of, 58
    rhythm (calendar), 12, 26, 49,
        54–55
    sympto-thermal, 12, 54

temperature, 52–54
withdrawal (coitus interruptus),
    12, 26, 55
Fibroids, 44, 125, 130, 179, 211
Filshie clip, 229
Fimbria, 31
Foams, 81, 82
Follicle-stimulating hormone (FSH),
    32–33, 118
Food and Drug Administration
    (FDA), 64, 72, 101, 115, 143,
    152, 156, 164, 206, 207, 210,
    212–13, 221, 222, 228
French abortion pill (RU486),
    210–12, 221

Gallbladder disease, 128
Genital area, external, 27–28
Genital warts, 21, 24, 67
Gestodene, 127
Gonadotropin-releasing hormone
    (GnRH), 32
Gonorrhea, 21, 24, 67, 95
Gossypol, 232
Granuloma, 198
Granulosa cells, 33

Hair loss, 153, 164
HDL (high-density lipoprotein),
    163
Headaches, 126, 131, 140, 142, 153
Health conditions
    contraceptive choice and, 25,
        43–44
    hormone-based methods and, 43,
        116, 127–29, 132, 139–40,
        154
Heart disease, 128, 139, 152, 199
Hematoma, 198–99
Hepatitis B, 24
Herpes, 21, 58, 67, 95
HIV, 24, 42, 58, 63, 66, 76, 77, 95,
    123, 155
Hormone-based methods
    male contraceptives, 231–32
    patches, 231
    vaginal rings, 229–30
    See also Depo-Provera; Minipill,
        progestin-only; Norplant;
        Pill

Human papillomavirus (HPV), 21,
    44, 67
Hymen, 28
Hypertension, 132, 142
Hysterectomy, 26

Implanon, 143, 228
Implants
    research on, 143, 228
    See also Norplant
Infertility
    factors in, 20, 21
    IUD and, 172, 179
Inserts, 81
Intrauterine devices (IUDs), 1, 9,
    40–41, 42, 146, 169–80
    age of users, 18, 19
    candidates for, 178–80
    cost of, 14, 173
    effectiveness of, 12, 105, 147, 173
    extended use of, 172, 174
    health conditions and, 44
    and infection risk, 172, 175–76,
        225
    insertion of, 171–72
    morning-after, 207–8
    operation of, 171
    popularity of, 26, 169
    pros and cons of, 15, 173–76
    research on, 225–27
    reversibility of, 176
    safety and side effects of, 176–78
In-vitro fertilization (IVF), 190
IUDs. See Intrauterine devices

Jaundice, 131, 132
Jellies, 81, 82

Labia majora, 27
Labia minora, 27
Lactational amenorrhea method
    (LAM), 12
Lamb-intestine condoms, 64, 67, 68
Laparoscopy, 185–86, 191
Laparotomy, 187
Late abortions, 209–10
Latex
    cervical caps, 10, 108
    condoms, 64, 70, 71, 105
    diaphragms, 90, 97

LDL (low-density lipoprotein), 117,
    126
Lea's Shield, 224, 225
Levonorgestrel-T (LNG-20) IUD,
    225, 226
Lifestyle, and contraceptive choice,
    14–16
Litigation, as deterrent to birth
    control research, 220
Liver cancer, 128, 132
Liver disease, 43, 162
Luteinizing hormone (LH), 33, 34,
    118

Melasma, 126
Men
    attitude toward birth control,
        23, 71
    contraceptives for, 231–33
    See also Condoms; Vasectomy
Menarche, 37
Menopause, 26
Menstrual cycle, 31–32, 56
    breastfeeding and, 35–36
    events of, 32–34
    personal history of, 40–41
    variations in, 36–37, 55
    See also Bleeding
Menstrual extraction, 209
Mestranol, 116
Methotrexate, 35, 212–13
Mifepristone (RU486), 210–12, 221
Migraine, 153
Minilaparotomy, 186, 192
Minipill, progestin-only, 116,
    133–42
    candidates for, 141–42
    cost of, 136
    effectiveness of, 136
    manufacturers of, 133
    operation of, 134
    pill-taking regimen, 134–36
    popularity of, 133
    pros and cons of, 136–38
    reversibility of, 138–39
    safety and side effects of, 139–41
Misoprostol, 212–13
Monogamy
    mutual, 66
    serial, 42

Mons pubis, 27
Morning-after IUD, 207–8
Morning-after pill, 205, 206–7,
    253
Multiload Cu375 IUD, 226
Mutual monogamy, 66

National Cancer Institute (NCI),
    128, 129
National Institutes of Health (NIH),
    199–200, 221, 222
National Survey of Family Growth,
    4, 50
Natural birth control. See Fertility
    awareness methods
Nausea, hormone-based methods
    and, 125–26, 130, 140, 142,
    153
New Drug Application (NDA),
    228
New England Journal of Medicine,
    4, 56, 212
Nonoxynol-9, 81, 224
Norethindrone, 134
Norgestimate, 116, 127, 227
Norgestrel, 134
Norplant, 9, 42, 43, 95, 143–55, 220,
    250
    candidates for, 154–55
    cost of, 13, 14, 146–47
    effectiveness of, 12, 13, 105, 146
    extended use of, 149, 151
    insertion of, 145–46, 151
    manufacturers of, 143
    operation of, 144–45
    partner's attitude toward, 23
    popularity of, 143
    pros and cons of, 15, 16, 147–50
    research on, 228
    reversibility of, 150–51
    safety and side effects of, 151–54
    side effects of, 31
Novagard, IUD, 226

Octoxynol, 82
Oral contraceptives. See Minipill,
    progestin-only; Pill
Oral sex, condom protection in,
    66, 68
Orgasm, 55

Ortho Annual Birth Control Study,
    1, 4, 26, 50, 63, 82, 89, 115,
    143, 156, 169, 193
Ortho-Novum 7/7/7, 117
Os, 30
Osteoporosis, Depo-Provera and,
    163
Ovarian cancer, 25, 43, 122, 128,
    130, 154
Ovarian cysts, 122, 140, 152
Ovaries, 31, 32, 33
Oviducts. See Fallopian tubes
Ovulation, 33–34, 36, 56, 93
    hormone-based methods and, 14,
    118, 119, 145, 157
Ovulation method. See Cervical
    mucus method

Pap smear, 30, 44, 107–8, 111
ParaGard IUD, 171, 172, 173, 174,
    175, 176, 179, 225
Patches, 231
Pelvic inflammatory disease (PID),
    21, 44, 95, 122, 123, 138, 149,
    161, 164, 175, 179
Personality, and contraceptive
    choice, 14–16
Pharmaceutical companies, 222–23
Phenobarbital, 140
Phenytoin, 140
Physicians Desk Reference (PDR),
    4, 115, 253
Pill, 9, 31, 32, 43, 95, 115–42, 219
    age of users, 17, 18, 19
    brand names of, 115
    candidates for, 129–32
    cost of, 14, 121
    drug interactions with, 127
    effectiveness of, 12, 66, 121
    emergency, 12
    estrogen and progestin levels in,
    116–17, 125
    health benefits of, 25, 43, 122, 123,
    128, 130
    health risks of, 43, 116, 127–29,
    132
    low-dose, 116, 117–18, 125
    missed pills, 120
    morning-after, 205, 206–7, 253
    operation of, 118

Pill *(cont'd)*
  partner's attitude toward, 23
  pill-taking regimen, 118–20
  popularity of, 26, 115
  pros and cons of, 121–23
  research on, 227–28
  reversibility of, 123–24
  side effects of, 117–18, 124–26, 131
  tips for taking, 130
  See also Minipill, progestin-only
Pituitary gland, 118
Placebo, 118
Placenta, 34
Political climate, as deterrent to birth control research, 220–21
Polyurethane condoms, 64, 67, 71, 72, 78
Population Council, 5, 211, 223
Pregnancy
  conception and, 32–34, 36–37
  ectopic (tubal), 34–35, 140, 152, 177–78
  with IUD in place, 176, 177
  unintended, 178, 203–4, 213–14
  See also Birth control failure
Pregnancy tests, home, 204–5
Premenstrual syndrome (PMS), 164
Prentif Cavity-Rim cervical cap, 101
Progestasert IUD, 171, 172, 173, 174, 225
Progesterone, 33, 34, 116
Progestin-estrogen methods. *See* Pill; Vaginal ring
Progestin-only methods. *See* Depo-Provera; Minipill, progestin-only; Norplant; Vaginal ring
Prolactin, 35
Prostaglandin, 210, 211, 212
Prostate cancer, and vasectomy, 199–200
Pulmonary embolism, 127

Reality female condom. *See* Condoms, female
Reproductive organs, 29–31
Rhythm (calendar) method, 12, 26, 49, 54–55

Rifampin, 127, 140, 153
RU486 (mifepristone), 210–12, 221

Scrotum, 195
Semen, 195
Serial monogamy, 42
Sexual behavior
  and contraceptive choice, 42–43
  mutual monogamy, 66
  serial monogamy, 42
  after vasectomy, 200
Sexually transmitted diseases (STDs), 42–43, 58, 122–23, 138, 149, 161, 173, 174, 179, 188, 189, 198
  condom (female) protection for, 76, 123
  condom (male) protection for, 42, 66, 68, 123
  diaphragm protection for, 95
  information sources on, 247–48
  risk of, 20–22, 24, 175
  spermicide protection for, 84–85, 224
  vaginal discharge in, 51–52
Sickle-cell disease, 164
Skin patches, 231
Smoking, hormone-based methods and, 128, 132
Sperm, 194, 195
  antibodies, 199
  frozen before vasectomy, 197
  suppression drugs, 231–32
  survival of, 36, 37
Spermicides, 31, 43, 81–88
  age of users, 18, 19
  birth defects and, 86, 97
  candidates for, 88
  with cervical caps, 102, 103, 105
  with condoms, 67, 68, 69, 84
  cost of, 13, 14, 84–85
  with diaphragms, 83, 90, 93–94, 95, 96, 97, 98–99
  effectiveness of, 12, 83–84
  forms of, 81–82
  instructions for using, 82–83
  pros and cons of, 85–86
  research on, 224
  reversibility of, 86

safety and side effects of, 84, 86, 88, 95, 97
STD protection of, 84, 85
tips for using, 87
Sponges, 12, 14, 26, 81, 82, 223–24
Statistical information, sources of, 4–5
STDs. *See* Sexually transmitted diseases
Sterilization. *See* Tubal ligation; Vasectomy
Stroke, 127, 132, 139
Suction curettage (vacuum aspiration), 208–9, 214
Suppositories, 81
Surfactants, 82
Sympto-thermal methods, 54
Syphilis, 24

Temperature method, 52–54
Testicles, 194–95, 199
Testosterone, in male contraceptive, 232
Thermometers, basal, 52, 57
Thromboembolism (blood clots), 127–28, 139, 152
Thrombophlebitis (blood clots), 43, 132, 152, 162
Toxic shock syndrome (TSS)
cervical cap and, 103, 108, 109, 110
diaphragm and, 99
Trichomoniasis, 51
Triphasic pill, 117, 118, 126
Tubal ligation (sterilization), 183–92
age of users, 17, 18, 19
candidates for, 192
cost of, 13
effectiveness of, 12, 187–88
electrocautery, 185, 190
laparoscopy, 185–86, 188, 191
laparotomy, 187
minilaparotomy, 186, 192
popularity of, 26, 183
postpartum, 186, 187
pros and cons of, 188–89

research on, 229
reversibility of, 189–90
safety and side effects of, 190–92
Tubal pregnancy. *See* Ectopic pregnancy

Urethra, 28
Urinary tract infections, diaphragm and, 97, 99
Urologist, 195
Uterine cancer, 154
Uterus, 29, 30, 31, 32, 33, 208, 209

Vaccine, contraceptive, 231
Vacuum aspiration (suction curettage), 208–9, 213
Vagina, 28, 29, 30
sores in, 84, 95
Vaginal contraceptive film (VCF), 81, 82
Vaginal discharge, 51–52, 58
Vaginal rings, 229–30
Vaginal spermicides. *See* Spermicides
Vaginal suppository, 26
Vas deferens, 194–95, 198
Vasectomy (sterilization), 193–200
age of users, 17, 18, 19
candidates for, 200
cost of, 13, 188, 196
effectiveness of, 12, 196
popularity of, 26, 193
pros and cons of, 197–98
recovery from, 195–96
research on, 232
reversibility of, 198
safety and side effects of, 198–200
surgical procedure in, 194–95
Vulva, 27

Water retention, 126
Weight gain, 126, 140, 160–61, 164
Withdrawal, 12, 26, 55
World Health Organization (WHO), 164, 232

Yuzpe regimen, 206

ABOUT THE AUTHORS

JENNIFER CADOFF is a highly respected medical writer whose articles have appeared in leading women's magazines, including *Allure, Glamour, McCall's, Mirabella, New Woman*, and *Redbook*, and in the parenting magazines *Parents* and *Child*. An article she wrote for *Glamour* was nominated for a National Magazine Award in 1994. Before becoming a freelance writer, Ms. Cadoff worked for more than ten years as a magazine editor. Most recently, she held the position of health director at *Self* magazine. Prior to that, she worked at *Mademoiselle* as a writer and an editor in the health department.

SAMUEL A. PASQUALE, M.D., is an internationally known leader in birth control research. He is currently professor of obstetrics and gynecology and reproductive science, as well as chief of women's health research, at Robert Wood Johnson Medical School, which is part of the University of Medicine and Dentistry of New Jersey. Dr. Pasquale has been actively involved in contraceptive research for over thirty years. While at Robert Wood Johnson, he has been a principal investigator in the research and development of several of today's latest birth control methods leading to their approval by the FDA, including Norplant, Norplant 2, and Ortho Cyclen oral contraceptives. He has published numerous articles on contraception in medical journals. In the past Dr. Pasquale has worked at several major pharmaceutical companies in the area of contraceptive research and development, and he holds a number of patents for multiphasic contraceptives.